Before It's Too Late

Employee Involvement...
An Idea Whose Time Has Come

Peter B. Grazier

Teambuilding, Inc.
Chadds Ford, Pennsylvania

Published by
Teambuilding, Inc.
12 Pine Lane
Chadds Ford, Pennsylvania 19317
(215) 358-1961

Designed, Edited and Typeset by
Martin Unlimited
2 Marineview Plaza, Box 5E
Hoboken, New Jersey 07030
(201) 798-0298

Printed by
Farley Printing Company, Inc.
115 South Justison Street
Wilmington, Delaware 19801

Cover Design by
Guy Tenaro of Farley Printing Company, Inc.

9 8 7 6 5 4 3
FIRST EDITION

ISBN 0-9622232-0-4
Printed in the United States of America

Before It's Too Late

Acknowledgments

In the course of writing a book, and indeed, even gaining the courage to attempt it, one has to realize that others play a part. There are many who have unknowingly participated in the development of this book, but it is impossible to list them all. However, I would like to call special attention to some who have particularly influenced my thinking, and without whom my work might have taken a different course. My deepest gratitude to:

John C. "Cub" Ronquest, who showed me how to eliminate confrontation from the workplace. Frank Hendrickson (now deceased), who gave me the opportunity to experiment. Dr. Richard Tucker, who helped to shape my thinking about employee involvement in the workplace. Tom Peters, who helped me shift business thinking from left brain to right brain. Dr. Wayne Dyer, whose work on achieving maximum human potential has helped me (and my clients) more than he will ever know. Pierre R. H. Landrieu, who has enabled me to continue to evolve. My brother, Steve, who has always encouraged me to strive for a better workplace, and also reviewed my manuscript. My mother, Vivian Grazier, who taught me that all people have value. And particularly, my wife, Barbara, for sticking by me through all my wacky ideas.

Additionally, I would like to thank those who graciously gave their time to review my manuscript and share their ideas: Karen Wydra, Laura Robinson, Phil and Dolly Schulman, Ron and Mariah Gladis, Valerie Herman, Dr. Barry Axe, Joe Banachowski, Bill McCune, and Dr. Rob Gilbert. And finally I would like to thank Irene Frankel and David Martin for their excellent advice and assistance in the final assembly of this book.

To the American workforce

Contents

Introduction

Employee involvement. The term is being used more frequently as the need for improving our organizations becomes greater. It's a concept that sounds ridiculously simple: soliciting input from employees at all levels of an organization about ways to solve problems and improve performance.

Dramatic improvements in virtually all aspects of business are possible when organizations implement employee involvement concepts. Such organizations as Harley-Davidson, Inc., Weirton Steel Corporation, The New United Motors Manufacturing, Inc., Preston Trucking, Pennsylvania Department of Transportation, Florida Power & Light, and Ford Motor Company have had enormous successes attributable to employee involvement efforts.

And, as most people will agree, involving employees in decision-making is an effective way to address today's concerns of employee motivation and morale.

Yet, a survey of employee involvement programs around the country reveals that **most employee involvement efforts fail within a year of implementation.**

Why?

Many reasons are cited. Poor management-labor relations; insufficient training; middle-management resistance; major disruptions, such as lay-offs; union resistance, and so

1

forth. The leading cause of failure, however, is **insufficient management commitment and support.**

But why would a concept that so clearly produces results <u>not</u> receive total management commitment and support?

To begin with, too often management undertakes these pro-grams with the simplistic view of employee involvement as a "quick fix," a feedback mechanism, an idea generator. So when employees begin questioning procedures that don't work, or begin raising issues about working hours and shift schedules, the work environment, budgets, project schedules, and other issues traditionally in management's domain, the effort caves in under the weight of management ego and insecurity.

The affected managers and supervisors have not been prepared for the change, so they resist. They don't expect front-line employees to be so concerned and frustrated about these issues or so interested in the company and its success. The outpouring of employee concerns catches them off-guard. The long lists of "problems" generated by front-liners overwhelm even the best of managers. They honestly hadn't realized there were so many problems needing attention.

So should it surprise us if these managers feel uncomfort-able about worker participation? Once, after his new employ-ee involvement team had brainstormed a long list of problems in his group, a manager said to me, "What if my boss sees this list? He's going to wonder what <u>I'm</u> doing!" Is his apprehension justified? Or is this just the paranoia of a timid and insecure upper-middle manager?

In fact, this manager runs one of the better departments in his company. In addition, he is respected by his people, who see him as knowledgeable and competent. Nevertheless, he's very uncomfortable with the concerns being raised by

2

his team. And without someone or something to help him through this discomfort, he'll probably resist the further use of his employee team...the source of the discomfort.

Participative management/employee involvement is a frequently misunderstood concept. Are we turning the company over to the employees? Are we now ruling by committee? Do I consult with my subordinates on all future decisions? Am I giving up authority? These are just a few of the questions raised by senior and middle managers and front-line supervisors when the concepts are introduced.

When we combine our egos and insecurities, our expectations of management's role, and our cultural biases and values with our natural resistance to change, the probability of resistance goes up significantly.

The purpose of this book is to bring some of these issues to light...to create a better understanding of employee involvement so that managers will not just support it, but will make it an active part of their management styles.

And, as you will see, employee involvement is no longer a "nice to do" concept. It is a philosophy of management that must be adopted if American business is to survive in our dramatically changing world. We simply must use all resources available to us, and the human mind, with its infinite capacity for creativity, imagination, and ingenuity, is a resource of enormous proportion.

1 What Is Employee Involvement?

*Western philosophy says that work exists to provide
goods and services...Eastern philosophy says that work
exists to enhance the human spirit.*

On a construction project in St. Louis, Missouri, work was progressing slowly on a complicated "clean" room to be used for manufacturing high-grade silicon for computer chips. The project manager was concerned that delays constructing this room would soon cause the entire construction schedule to fall behind. There was just too much work to be done by too many workers in too small a space.

Part of the work was the installation of 150 air duct connections into a main duct located in the ceiling. There were only five days to install the 150 connections, but the amount of working space in the room limited the number of sheetmetal workers to two.

The project manager, superintendent, and engineer concluded that it would take an extraordinary effort for two workers to accomplish the job. But how would they approach two union construction workers so they would put out this extraordinary effort?

The project manager finally said, "Have the foreman choose two men and send them to my office." When the men arrived, they weren't quite sure what the project manager wanted. After all, construction craftsworkers are

5

never invited to the boss's office—except, that is, for disciplinary measures.

On the wall of the office was a drawing of the 150 duct connections. "Fellows," the project manager said, "could you tell us if it's possible for two men to install these 150 connections in five days?"

The two sheetmetal workers first looked at the drawing on the wall, then looked at each other. Then one of them took a pencil and made five circles on the drawing, each encompassing 30 connections, and representing how much work would have to be done each day. The men looked at each other again and then said to the manager, "We're not sure, but let us try." Four and a half days later the work was complete, and the "clean" room remained on schedule.

Jean, a cost clerk in the planning and budgeting department of a large organization, had an attitude toward work that was considerably less than enthusiastic.

When management asked for volunteers for her group's work performance team, Jean signed up. She figured the hour and a half meeting each week would, at least, be a break from her routine.

Along with her team members, Jean was given training in problem-solving and interpersonal skills. Over the next few months, Jean's team succeeded in making changes that significantly improved the work performance and morale in her department. During this time, there was a noticeable improvement in Jean's appearance and attitude.

For their next project, the team members chose Jean to be their new leader. Having listened and learned well, she became a model team leader and successfully guided them through the project.

6

Jean's poise and skills were noticed by a high level manager. As a result, Jean was transferred to another group and promoted from clerical to management. Jean also began organizing social outings for the company on a volunteer basis, and ultimately received an award of appreciation from her fellow employees.

Jim was a shop steward at a large manufacturing facility. He was recruited to be a member of a task force that was to recommend ways to solve a significant parking problem.

Jim's attitude was adversarial and negative. During the first two meetings he sat back with arms crossed and said nothing. His value to the team was zero.

The enthusiasm of the other members, however, was infectious, and during the third meeting Jim began to inject a few words here and there. By the fourth meeting he was fully involved.

The team realized they would have to obtain the support of the local union if their recommendations were to have any chance of success. Jim offered to work with the union as his contribution to the team effort, and succeeded in gaining the union's support for the parking project.

During the final meeting, when the group was almost ready to disband, Jim proposed that the team send thank you letters to all the people (primarily engineers) who had provided assistance. No one else had thought of it. It was a great idea.

Several months later, Jim volunteered and was accepted as a member of the company's recognition committee, responsible for identifying deserving employees and giving them awards.

What do these three people have in common? All three were positively affected by becoming <u>involved</u> in their organization's work. All three underwent a transformation in behavior as a result of being treated as people with value.

These three stories are all true. They are three out of the hundreds of similar experiences we've witnessed in the last eight years that were a direct result of a concept called <u>Employee Involvement</u>.

What is Employee Involvement? It's a way of engaging employees at all levels in the thinking processes of an organization. It's the recognition that many decisions made in an organization can be made better by soliciting the input of those who may be affected by the decision. It's an understanding that people at all levels of an organization possess unique talents, skills, and creativity that can be of significant value if allowed to be expressed.

Although employee involvement is often associated with work teams such as quality circles, any situation involving an employee in some decision becomes employee involvement—as long as management sincerely considers the ideas being offered. A one-on-one discussion between a supervisor and subordinate can be employee involvement. A suggestion program can be employee involvement. A "brown bag" luncheon between front-line workers and the vice president can be employee involvement. A weekly staff meeting that encourages dialogue can be employee involvement.

The form it takes is less important than the principle involved. The message sent by management in any employee involvement interaction is, "You have value. You have talent, skill, and creativity. You are important, and I need your help." This message contains the power to change lives and organizations.

8

The Popularity of Small Group Problem-Solving

From about 1970 on, with the adoption of Japanese management concepts, American businesses began using small groups of employees for problem-solving and idea-generating. The primary reason for the popularity of this approach is that many more and better ideas can be generated from "mind pooling."

The human brain stores billions of thought impulses that are not always easily retrieved. A "best solution" to a problem may be locked away in someone's mind, but the person either doesn't know it or can't retrieve it. The person needs a catalyst. In a group of people, the catalyst is provided by someone else's thought. One thought triggers another, releasing more and more ideas. And since people in a group tend to build on each other's thoughts, the ideas and ultimate solutions of the group are better than the individual's idea alone.

In addition to mind-pooling, the group process serves an even greater value: it builds trust, confidence, skills, and teamwork.

When employees are initially introduced to employee involvement concepts, although interested and excited about their involvement, they are unsure about their ability to produce meaningful results. They understandably feel a certain amount of insecurity. But when they are part of a group, their insecurity is lessened. They now have fellow members who provide other skills that will enhance the probability of success.

Members learn from each other and grow in their ability to lead teams, solve complex problems, and interact with others. They learn about the business of the company, and, particularly, that the solutions to all those problems they've been complaining about are not as easy as they thought. **They gain a new appreciation for management.**

But It Takes Longer With a Team

When we introduce the small group process of problem-solving, we invariably hear the objection, "It takes too long." There's no question that involving more people in the solution of a problem takes longer. In fact, when we train teams, we run an exercise that shows exactly that.

The exercise sets up the following scenario: a crew of astronauts, whose module has crashed on the moon, needs to get to the mother ship, 200 miles away. There's a list of 15 items they salvaged from the module to help them on their journey. Among the items on the list are a first aid kit, a pistol, matches, a stellar map, a compass, and two tanks of oxygen.

We first ask everyone as **individuals** to rank-order the items from most important to least important. The participants usually take from seven to eight minutes to complete the list.

Then we ask the participants to form teams of five or six members and to rank-order the items again **as a team**. The participants get into lively, sometimes heated, discussions about the items, and it usually takes each team from 15 to 20 minutes to complete the list.

At the end, we score all lists according to an ideal ranking suggested by NASA. In at least 97% of the cases, **the**

10

scores of the teams are significantly better than the scores of the individuals. The exercise confirms that it does take longer to make a decision through a team approach. But the quality of the answer is significantly better.

This exercise has a profound effect on the participants because it clearly demonstrates the enormous power of people working collaboratively rather than individually. And therein lies the secret of the popularity of the small group method of problem solving.

Input Only...or Some Control?

So far we've talked about employee involvement in terms of providing **input** to the decision making process. But what about control? Do we actually start turning over more control of the organization to front-line employees?

Making people responsible for their work implies giving them some authority to make corrections where needed. When employees begin to look at their work for ways to improve it, they'll find that minor adjustments and corrections may be needed that don't merit a full-blown presentation to management.

Take, for example, the implementation of Statistical Process Control in manufacturing settings. Traditionally, machine operators push buttons without being concerned about quality control; further down the line, the quality controller catches any defects in the manufacturing process. With SPC, machine operators are given the training and tools to monitor the quality of their work. If the machine operators find that product specifications are not being met,

11

they have the power to take independent action and shut down the process so the correction can be made.

The perception of "giving up some control" is really a **misperception** shared by many managers. In fact, by giving up some control, we are actually gaining more control.

We have been trained in America to think that managers maintain control over all activity in their departments. It, therefore, becomes difficult for some managers to step back and delegate more authority to front-liners. But managers who are working successfully with employee involvement are finding that as they turn over more control of day-to-day work operations and decisions to front-liners, they gain more time to plan, assess progress, and work with customers. Any manager who has complained, "I don't have time to plan," will see the obvious benefit of delegating some authority.

In fact, delegating authority is likely to become a necessity, not an option. Significant changes in American business brought on by world competition are forcing us to reduce layers of management. Managers will find themselves responsible for many more people, and it will be impossible for managers to know what each employee is doing all the time. Managers will have to depend on front-liners to use sound judgment in solving their own problems.

So the answer to the "control" question is yes, managers are, in a sense, giving up some control. By referring responsibility and decision-making to lower levels, managers do yield some measure of control. But in another sense, managers are actually gaining more control by freeing themselves from the minutiae, allowing time for more important concerns.

A Culture Change

Many of us who worked with employee involvement years ago naively regarded it as a management tool...another technique in the arsenal of management concepts to improve organizations. But as we observed its initial success, then the resistance to it, then its failure, we wondered why something that so clearly produced results was failing.

What we discovered was our own shortsightedness in **not recognizing the effect of employee involvement on the culture of the organization.** What we had perceived as "merely getting people involved in problem-solving" turned out to be a major change in the way we managed our workforce.

For years, managers have been told that their jobs were to produce a product or service. They were responsible for the production, quality, costs, schedules, and ideas for improvement.

But managers weren't told that their jobs were also to encourage and motivate their workers to be concerned with these things, let alone involve them. So when employees began raising issues about poor work procedures, outdated reports, the need for training, department goals, and so on, the managers said, "Wait a minute! That's my job!" or "Who are they to question the way I run my department?" And as the level of discomfort rose, so did the number of program failures.

It became obvious that employee involvement was not "just getting people involved in problem-solving." We came to realize it was a major change in the way most organizations operate.

Any organization moving to a participative management philosophy must, therefore, consider the cultural implications and plan for them accordingly. We will discuss implementation further in Chapter 6.

A Final Word

So what is employee involvement? It's a "common sense" philosophy of management that encourages everyone in the organization to be part of the decision-making process so the organization continuously improves.

It's not something "nice" we do for our employees to make them feel better. It's an understanding that it's everyone's obligation—part of the job—to constantly look for better ways of doing things. It's part of the job to ask questions and raise issues of concern, to get them out on the table so they can be resolved. How else can we get better?

Above all, employee involvement is not simply another management tool, but a major change of direction in the way we lead our workforce. It's a change that affects the culture of the workplace as we've come to know it in this century, and, therefore, it's a change that must be implemented with great care and attention.

2 So Why Change?

Gentlemen, we must all hang together, else we shall,
most assuredly, all hang separately.

—Benjamin Franklin,
at the signing of the Declaration of Independence

Change. The psychologists say change frightens us. They say we like predictability in our world, and change interferes with our ability to predict how things will be. So, as best we can, we resist it.

But the irony is that our world is constantly changing, and with respect to technology, changing at an increasingly rapid pace. John Naisbett, in his bestseller *Megatrends*, points out that it took America 100 years to move from an agricultural society to an industrial society, but only **twenty years** to move from an industrial to an information society.[1] In 1950, new businesses were being created at the rate of 93,000 a year; in 1984, at the rate of more than 600,000 per year.[2] The rate of change is astonishing, and in some cases bewildering.

Yet even with the significant changes around us, many of our businesses are slow to react. Why does "business as usual" still seem to be the norm? Perhaps because the need to change is not strong enough.

Before any meaningful change can occur in anything, people must feel a need to change. There must be some pain, or dissatisfaction with the status quo. But apparently most

15

Americans are not feeling this pain, and therefore, see no need to change the way we work. Some, notably in the smokestack industries, have felt it. But most still have not. Most businesses are still profitable and surviving; most Americans still enjoy a reasonably comfortable standard of living. So what will be the stimulus, the drive to change the way we work and behave in our society and workplace? What will provide the impetus to move more Americans toward giving more of themselves and their productive capacity to their work? Maybe a discussion of the dismal facts facing our country is in order.

The Ugly Facts

- Americans no longer enjoy the world's highest standard of living. We now trail Sweden, Denmark, West Germany, Switzerland, Holland, and Norway.[3]
- The United States ranks **last** among the industrialized nations in the rate of productivity growth.[4]
- The United States has the highest percentage of obsolete plants, the lowest percentage of capital investment, and the lowest growth of savings of any major industrial country.[5]
- Among the nations of Japan, France, Netherlands, Australia, Belgium, Italy, Germany, and the United States, only the U.S. has a capital gains tax.[6]
- There are now 86 countries in the world that have auto assembly lines.[7]
- In Japan it takes an auto worker 11 hours to build a car; in the United States, 31 hours.[8]
- In 1980, Japan became the number one automobile producer in the world, exceeding U. S. production by 40%.

- In 1978, the average Japanese steel worker produced 421 tons of steel while his counterpart in America produced 250.[9]
- Between 1970 and 1988, our share of the USA's consumer electronics market fell from 100% to under 5%.[10]
- In 1966, 45,000 patents were granted to U.S. inventors by foreign countries; in 1976, 15,000. By contrast, the number of patents granted by the United States to foreign inventors rose from 14,000 to 26,000.[11]
- America's high school SAT (Scholastic Aptitude Test) scores went down steadily for 20 years. Even though these scores have gone up some in recent years, they are still below the levels of 1965.[12]
- As of 1982, Japan graduates more engineers per year than the United States.[13]
- In 1965, the United States had three times the number of engineers and scientists as did Japan. Now Japan has more.[14]
- From 1975 to 1988, America's trade balance went from a positive $9 billion to a negative $161 billion.[15]
- In 1985, for the first time in this century, the U.S. joined the company of nations in debt. By 1986, foreign debt had reached $250 billion, making us the largest debtor nation in the world.[16]
- Among the major industrialized nations, the United States ranks worst in government spending as a percent of GNP.[17]
- In the 1980s, the federal deficit has almost quadrupled from $60 billion to $220 billion in 1986.[18]
- Just containing defense procurement cost **overruns** to half their amount during the last decade would have given us enough money to maintain the necessary military postures, save our ailing auto and other

industries, rebuild decaying cities, and refurbish our public transportation system.[19]

- When Medicare legislation was enacted in 1965, it was intended to cost the country $8 billion by 1990.[20] Today those estimates are approaching $100 billion.

As if all this weren't enough, America's service sector is now coming under siege. According to an April 1988 article in *USA Today*:

> The USA, which has already blown its lead in manufacturing, has proven to be just as vulnerable a target in service, the sector that provides 75% of our jobs in fields from banking and insurance to restaurants and retailing.

> In the first quarter, the USA's long-running trade surplus in services disappeared. **This year, the USA will have a trade deficit in services for the first time in 50 years.** That means the interest we pay foreigners for loans and investments, plus the dollars we spend on foreign-owned services, will exceed what we get from them.

> This downward spiral raises very serious questions about this nation's future. We have retreated from manufacturing to focus on service, which now accounts for 71% of the nation's GNP. If our service firms can't compete, then what can?[21]

Also in April 1988, *Inc.* magazine listed the top ten banks in the world (ranked by assets). As opposed to 15 years ago when the United States dominated the list, we now have **one bank** in the top ten. Japan has seven and France has two.[22] And our one bank just barely made the list!

The experts tell us that the single most significant determinant in maintaining our standard of living is productivity growth. Since the growth of productivity in America is last among the industrialized nations of the world, the experts again say our standard of living is declining and will continue declining as long as the problem persists.

But what does that mean to the average American? We still feel reasonably comfortable. What is this decline in standard of living they're talking about?

It means we pay more for everything we buy. It means our real incomes are less. It means our children might not be able to afford a new home by the year 2000. It means a college education will be too expensive for the average family. It means we don't eat meat as often each month. It means our vacations are less extravagant. It means taking the kids to one fewer hockey game next year. It means we shut down factories. It means more people out of work, and more people on welfare, which translates to a greater burden on those working.

A few years ago, former Federal Reserve Board Chairman Paul Volcker said, "I would point out that productivity growth in this country is actually negative...and of course we import 50% of our oil so that the higher revenues going abroad do not go to American citizens. Under these conditions **the standard of living of the average American has got to decline.** I don't think we can escape that when we are producing less with the same amount of effort."[23]

C. Jackson Grayson of the American Productivity Center says, "The crisis is real. For any leader the time to worry is when your speed is slower than the horses coming up behind you. The time to worry is not **after** but **before** they pass you by."[24]

19

If all this sounds bad, it is. These facts tell a story that Americans have been unwilling to hear. They are symptoms of a problem of gigantic proportions—a problem we'll eventually have to face. It's like the man selling the Fram oil filters who says, "You can pay me now, or you can pay me later."

In our organizations today—including our governments—an ever-present sense of comfort and well-being is lulling us into a false sense of security. Feeling comfortable and secure, we seem content to put in our normal four- or five-hour day.

We've had these ugly facts around us for years, yet we don't seem to be overly concerned. Will it take zero percent raises, salary cuts, or job lay-offs before we get the message?

If, in fact, people are hearing the message, it doesn't seem to be translating into concrete actions on the shop floor, in the typing pool, at the drafting board, at staff desks, or, unfortunately, in the manager's office.

How many of our employees, as they walk into work, think to themselves "How can I improve my job today?" or "How can I improve my company today?" or "What can I personally do to make this a better organization?" And how many managers encourage employees to take on this kind of responsibility?

To survive and maintain our way of life as we know it, we must change the way we work. We need to renew our sense of purpose, and instill in all a sense of urgency about our productivity. We need to place responsibility for the success of our organizations on all employees, not just on a handful of managers. And we need to understand that if all employees are to be responsible, they must be more fundamentally involved in the organization.

We simply have to pull out all the stops to generate ideas for improvement. We have to instill a sense of urgency in addressing the issue of quality. And we have to develop a national commitment to giving more to our jobs. The standards of the past won't hold up any more.

To demonstrate clearly the positive effects of creating a national focus on these serious issues, we need only to look at our toughest competitor, Japan.

Japan:

- Has the lowest crime rate in the world.
- Has the lowest unemployment rate in the world.
- Has the highest average life expectancy.
- Has the best transportation and commuter systems.
- Leads the world in patents.
- Has the toughest pollution control standards.
- Ranks first in scores on international achievement tests of science and math taken by schoolchildren.
- Has the highest percentage of students completing high school.
- Has the highest literacy rate.

Is it any wonder that we have witnessed the tremendous rate of growth of the Japanese economy and standard of living?

We simply must do something, and do it now.

Competition

In any free-market society, the primary motivation for change and improvement is competition. Competition spurs management on to re-evaluate the old way and move on to the new. And as we have moved from a national economy to a world economy, the competition has "heated up."

As a catalyst for change, foreign competition first hit the "smokestack" industries when steel and cars from Japan and Europe invaded America. As foreign technology improved, competition moved into "high tech" electronics. Now almost all audio and video equipment sold in America is made in other countries.

Competition has created pressure on business to focus on productivity and quality issues. Not only is the private sector affected; this increased pressure for performance has spread to the regulated industries, some of which now find themselves de-regulated.

The de-regulation of the airlines has wreaked havoc and wildly fluctuating fare structures. It has also brought corporate mergers and takeovers as one airline after another attempts to survive.

The de-regulation of the telephone companies has spawned several new companies, such as Sprint, MCI, and a host of regional companies, competing head-on with Ma Bell for long distance service and equipment.

The next change we anticipate is the de-regulation of the electric and gas utilities, which will find themselves in direct competition with smaller, private co-generation facilities owned by their most desired customers. These customers, in an attempt to lower energy costs, have installed their own small generating stations. Recent legislation now requires electric utilities to purchase any excess capacity from these units at a time when the utilities find themselves with their own excess capacity. In addition, future legislation is expected to ease the transmission of power across state borders, opening up the possibility of further competition among the utilities. Many of these utilities are now undergoing "belt-tightening" measures, such as cutbacks in personnel.

Perhaps the last hold-out will be our governments, which experience no direct threat to their profitability or survival. But as a contributor to the high cost of American business, federal, state, and local governments will eventually be pressured to look hard at their performance. They simply must reduce the mounds of paperwork required for businesses to operate so that business, in turn, can reduce overheads. It just doesn't make sense that, in a time when our businesses are struggling to survive, our government can turn a blind eye on its own cumbersome requirements.

As one industry after another has been threatened, managements have been forced to seek new strategies for survival. One of those strategies has been employee involvement.

Tom Peters, author of the best-selling book *In Search of Excellence*, has strongly emphasized that "the only three sustaining strategic distinctions are superior service, superior quality of product, and constant innovation. However, there is a fourth point, and that is obviously, or it should be obvious that, those three uniquely are built on a base of **participation by all hands.**"[25]

Competition and Quality

It would be a gross understatement to say that America is becoming interested in **quality**. It would be more accurate to say that Americans are becoming obsessed with it.

This obsession is not without cause. Japan has shown us that focusing on quality is certainly a good investment.

Also, marketing surveys have consistently shown that **relative perceived quality** is a major determinant of product or service success. People will happily and consistently pay much more for soft Charmin bathroom tissue than the local generic brand, and the lonely Maytag repairman is an appropriate symbol of his product's superiority. The next time you shop for a car, notice the premiums of $1000 to $2000 placed on Hondas and Toyotas...premiums that we are gladly paying to get such quality.

Also, we've begun to place better estimates on the **cost of quality**, documenting what poor quality costs us in lost productivity.

A primary thrust of this new quality consciousness is the **front-line employee**...the person best positioned to notice and correct quality deficiencies.

As we mentioned earlier, in manufacturing, we're teaching employees techniques such as Statistical Process Control (SPC), which empowers them to shut down their work stations when "out-of-spec" work is detected...a vast change from the "keep the lines rolling at all costs" mentality of just a few years ago.

Companies are also re-evaluating the role of the Quality Control Department with an eye towards delegating more responsibility for control to the employee making the product or providing the service. It has become painfully obvious that detection of problems "after the fact" is unacceptable in today's world.

So we now find the front-line worker playing a far more significant role in making quality more than just a word. Consider the young boy on the loading dock who makes a decision for quality when he decides <u>not</u> to drop the package. It clearly makes the point that our focus must be on employees at all levels.

24

Competition and Customers

When we look at competition, we need also to think about the Customer with a capital "C." Remember the most important measure of quality we discussed above? It was relative perceived quality. And guess who's doing the perceiving? The customer.

Probably at no time in the 200-year history of this country has the focus on the customer been as great as it is today. The phones don't ring, the product doesn't sell, and the company doesn't work if the customer can't be persuaded to buy.

Jan Carlzon, the dynamic head of the successful Scandinavian Airlines (SAS), is just one example of a leader who almost single-mindedly focuses the company's energy on the customer. And where does that energy come from? Employees.

Mr. Carlzon points out that every customer comes in contact with about five SAS employees. Multiply this by the 10 million customers who use their airline every year and you have, what he calls, 50 million "moments of truth"—50 million opportunities for employees to work magic on every customer.[26]

At the heart of any customer interaction is a **front-line employee.** The next time you're with a group of people, ask them all for a "customer horror story." We all have one. Let them tell you how some employee badgered, insulted, or degraded them, made them wait unnecessarily, or mishandled a request for information. Then ask them if they ever went back to that organization again. It's a sobering experience, and one that demonstrates the need for greater employee awareness of the customer.

Competition and Innovation

Look around you. More than likely you're in a room of some building. Look at all the "things" you can see: the floor, the walls, the ceiling...the furniture, light fixtures, doors...the light bulbs, switches, outlets...wall coverings, the colors, patterns, etc., etc., etc.

Consider that before any one of these was created, it resided as a **thought** in someone's mind. In fact, since the beginning of time, no object was ever made by a person that didn't first begin as a thought.

It's important to realize that humans, unlike other creatures, have an enormous capacity for **creative** thought. Within the power of the mind is the ability to create something that never before existed.

For some reason, in business today we don't think about this much. We go about our daily routine as though to exercise this creativity is not within our job scope. Or maybe we think it's someone else's job—the job of the research and development department, for example. And then we wonder as new and innovative foreign products and services flood our market. (Look at the facts on patents in the Ugly Facts section.)

While it's true that many companies have suggestion programs to get ideas from all employees, if you look at their results, you'll see numbers far below potential. An American company may be satisfied with 200, 1000 or even 5000 ideas submitted yearly. But compare these to the 100,000 or 200,000 ideas regularly seen by Toyota or Nissan, and the point becomes painfully clear. We simply do not put enough emphasis on innovation in America.

Most of the reason for this lack of emphasis on innovation stems from two basic sources.

First, the dominance of American products for most of this century has made us complacent. We simply have not had serious competition to force us to be more innovative.

Second, over the last 200 years, the growth of the American economy has emphasized efficient production above all else. The System of Mass Production begun by Eli Whitney in 1798 and refined by Henry Ford in 1906 made it unnecessary for average workers to use their minds. Performing simple, mundane operations day after day required no thinking on the part of workers...or so it seemed.

Around 1900 Frederick Taylor proposed his theory of Scientific Management.[27] Taylor suggested that management observe work operations and streamline them by reducing or simplifying steps in the process. Then workers would begin using the steps as outlined by management. In essence, management would do the thinking, and labor would do what management said.

While it's indisputable that we've made progress this century, in the process we've systematically defined the worker as an expendable tool, not a living, breathing, **thinking** being who brings to work each day the most sophisticated, educated, and well-informed mind that has ever existed in the history of civilization. In this process, we have also defined management as "the thinker."

Most management personnel today have grown up believing that workers are "the doers," and managers, "the thinkers." It's therefore difficult for some managers to accept a change toward more front-line worker input. And it's therefore not unusual for employee involvement practitioners to see managers get heartburn when workers suggest that an existing procedure doesn't work.

Those who have studied innovation have shown clearly that innovation is the result of a very spontaneous thought process, usually coming from the wrong person at the wrong time in the wrong place for the wrong reasons. Very rarely do innovations come about as a result of a planned effort.

If we look at how the human mind works, this will come as no surprise. In his book *The Mind*, Anthony Smith points out that "the human brain consists of ten to fifteen thousand million nerve cells. The number of synapses (nerve cell connections) is a thousand times more so, there being about one hundred million million of them."[28] The possible combinations of thought impulses from such a powerful tool is staggering.

The human mind is incredibly powerful and always working. So you can begin to understand the frustration workers experience on the job when not invited to "think" along with management.

A recent national survey asked workers "What do you want most in a job?" One of the most frequent responses was "A chance to use your mind and abilities," confirming today's workers' desire to contribute more to their work.

On a construction project once, a union carpenter who was hanging the ceiling wires for a very high suspended ceiling was having difficulty obtaining a mechanical "high-lift" to work from. Frustrated because he couldn't get the "high-lift," he devised a tool at the end of a long pole that would position the hanger wire and twist it into place. With this device he could hang the wires from the ground. The pro-

28

ductivity improvement was tremendous. Rental costs for additional high-lifts were avoided and a significant amount of time was saved.

I've seen this kind of thing happen hundreds of times when front-line workers are invited to participate with management in making something run better.

It's important to note that when construction projects end, the union craft workers are laid off and return to their union halls for the next available project. Workers may sit at home for weeks before being assigned a new job. By contributing ideas that improve productivity, work hours are reduced, causing the project to end sooner. This could be a strong disincentive to working productively.

In our experience, however, craft workers have had a strong desire to contribute their talents and creativity toward helping the job succeed, **even if it meant reducing their work.** This runs counter to the normally held beliefs about such workers, and is further confirmation of the desire of people to contribute in a positive way.

As a post-script to this story, the owner of the project was so impressed with the progress of the job and the attitude of the workers that new work was added to the contract, extending the work for another year. *What goes around comes around; what you give out, you get back.* The workers gave the best they had to offer, the owner gave them more work.

Innovation is badly needed for America to compete. Workers want to contribute with their minds and abilities. They only have to be asked.

Workforce

The workforce is changing—this much we know. But how it is changing and why is a source of bewilderment, irritation, frustration, and concern to many managers. "The work ethic is dead!" they say. "Why do we have to coddle today's workers? Why aren't workers happy to have a good job and a good salary?"

Personal Value Systems

Why do we fight? Why do we disagree? Why do so many of those young folks like that awful rock music? Why do some people believe in abortion while others don't? Why are some people prejudiced? Why do some people believe husbands and wives should share homemaking responsibilities equally, while others believe "a woman's place is in the home"? Why do some believe children should earn their allowance? Why do we go to war?

At the root of all this is our personal value system—**those beliefs we hold that help us to make judgments about the world around us**...those beliefs that help us to determine right from wrong, good from bad, or normal from not normal.[29]

According to Dr. Morris Massey of the University of Colorado, we develop about 90% of our value system during the first ten years of our life, and that value system drives much of our behavior the rest of our life. So to understand our beliefs, it helps to know what was going on around us those first few years, when we were "value programming."

During the implementation of an employee involvement effort in one organization, a particular senior manager had been subtly resisting for about a year. After a candid discussion about progress by top management, this manager wanted to talk with me alone.

He said he didn't like what was going on. "Why do we have to coddle today's workers anyway? Can't they be satisfied to come here just for a good job and good pay?"

I asked him when he was born. He said, "1927." I then asked him what was going on around him those first ten years of his life. He described "the Great Depression"—the sacrifices, deprivation, and hunger, all resulting from **no jobs and no money**. I explained to him that as a youngster observing and experiencing this, his value system placed importance on simply having a job and money to provide the basics of life.

I then contrasted this period with the post-war prosperity of the 50s and 60s. I asked him if he had any kids. He said he did. I then asked him if he had ever said to himself, "My kid's going to have it better. My kid's going to have the things I didn't get. My kid's going to get an education." He didn't answer, but his face told the answer. Sure he had, just like millions of other loving parents of the time.

I finally asked the manager if it was clearer to him that the expectations of today's workers, which go significantly beyond just having a job and good salary, were programmed in by his generation years ago. He agreed that it did make sense.

From that time on, it was easier to work with him. He no longer looked at today's younger workers as impudent upstarts, but as people whose values and resulting expectations were shaped by an entirely different set of circumstances. He didn't necessarily agree with their values, but he understood them better.

The 50s and 60s were a time when people were saying, "Let the little ones explore and ask questions. Don't control them too tightly. They'll be better adults." So these kids grew up asking lots of questions...and still are, which drives the older folks crazy.

Today's workers are asking a lot of questions, particularly, "Why do we do it this way?" Unfortunately, our business culture has fostered a management style that responds with, "Because that's the way I want it." Almost all managers will admit that inside they feel a twinge of anger when questioned about why something is needed, or why it's done a certain way.

At one large eastern electric utility, a committee of employees was assembled to assist management in solving problems in a 500-person department. In addressing employee concerns about "Information from Management," one of their recommendations was for managers to "explain the why's" when assigning work. Their rationale was that if they knew why something was needed, they would be in a better position to give the manager a better, more appropriate product.

In side conversations with some of the managers who heard this recommendation, it was obvious they were uncomfortable with it. Why should they have to explain themselves when assigning work?

In a very top-down, heavily management-directed organization, this kind of change is difficult. Even if management recognizes the need to share more information with the workforce, it is slow to move in that direction, and usually doesn't go far enough. And indications are that we may even be moving in the opposite direction.

Ongoing surveys by the Opinion Research Corporation in Princeton, New Jersey, have shown that employees believe their organizations are giving them less information. ORC surveys also show that employees feel that their organizations are losing touch with them, that they do a lousy job of encouraging suggestions for improvement, and that they are not responsive to problems and complaints.[30] Not surprisingly, employee attitudes sink to new lows.

By contrast, in a 1986 *Business Week*/Harris poll of middle managers of 600 corporations, 65% felt employees were **less loyal** than they were ten years ago.[31] Supporting this is a 1987 survey of 594 corporate managers by Uniforce Temporary Services showing that 65% believe that employee **work ethics and attitudes had changed for the worse.**

So while employees are feeling alienated from management, management thinks less highly of employees. And this at a time when our country needs the total cooperation and commitment of all hands!

Unions and the Workforce

Unions grew out of the belief that people were entitled to fair compensation and reasonable working conditions for their labor. Indeed, the union movement has been a major force in the rise of the standard of living of the average American.

But somewhere along the line, unions developed hierarchical structures of their own with many of the ills of a traditional management system. They have so much resembled big business that, in recent years, union members have felt alienated from their leadership.

Much of my work since 1974 has been with union-represented companies, and I have been appalled that organizations that purport to represent their members can be so out-of-touch with them. The union leadership simply hasn't been listening to their people.

In early work I did with union construction workers, for example, the workers expressed enormous frustration over America's poor performance in world competition. When I conducted orientations for new workers, many times the discussion of productivity would erupt into an outpouring of frustration. Improving productivity was a concern to them, but many of their negotiated work rules were counter-productive. As a result, we saw workers "break the rules" in order to improve productivity.

Another area where the union leadership has not been listening is in the four-day workweek. Probably 95% of the workers we talked with were anxious to work four ten-hour days a week instead of five eight-hour days. Most saw the four-day week as a way of having more time off from work and lower commuting costs.

But many union leaders wouldn't hear of it. They had worked hard to reduce a working day to eight hours, and they had no intention of "giving that up." The question is, is that representation?

It would be an oversimplification to state that this has caused the decline in union membership during the 70s and 80s. Certainly the shift from manufacturing to services has contributed to the decline. In 1985, *Business Week* reported, "Organized labor's share of the workforce is down to 19% and dropping fast. If this trend persists—and nothing on the horizon appears likely to change it—by the year 2000 unions will represent only 13% of all nonfarm workers."

But since unions still play an important role in our society, it was fortunate in 1985 that the AFL-CIO Executive Council agreed that they were out of step with the nation's changing workforce.

They decided that they should place at least as much emphasis on winning dignity and individual freedom for their members as they do on winning wage and benefit gains. "Today's workers," the Council noted, "may well be more interested in **having a say in the how, why and wherefore of their work** than they are in pay scales and benefit packages."[32] Again...employee involvement comes to the forefront.

This is a significant change of direction for America's organized labor leaders—one that may breathe life into a floundering labor movement.

America's Future
in World Competition

In January, 1985, the President's Commission on Industrial Competitiveness, a panel of government, business, academic, and labor leaders, presented its findings and recommendations to the President.[33]

In answer to the question, "Are we meeting the competitive challenge?" the Commission stated, "Not well enough. Our ability to compete in world markets is eroding. Growth in U.S. productivity lags far behind that of our foreign competitors. Real hourly compensation of our work force is no longer improving. U.S. leadership in world trade is declining."

The Commission went on to make four recommendations:
- **Create, apply, and protect technology.**
- Reduce the cost of capital to American industry.
- **Develop a more skilled, flexible, and motivated work force.**
- Make trade a national priority.

Two of these four recommendations dovetail with the goals of employee involvement, first to develop commitments toward national competitiveness and working together, then to make use of America's brainpower to create innovative and new technology.

The Commission further stated that "America's people—our most vital resource—are the drivers of our economy. Their vision, skill, and motivation are essential elements of our competitive potential. **The greatest competitive strategy in the world is doomed to failure if it lacks a dedicated team of players to carry it out.** Although great strides have been made over the last decade toward increased cooperation in some industries, **teamwork remains the exception rather than the rule.**"

The Commission's specific recommendation in this area stated, "American labor and management must move boldly to establish new cooperative relationships that will maximize productivity by involving employees and their elected representatives in decision-making in the work place, as well as encouraging participative management throughout the organization.

"In addition, the President should publicly recognize those cooperative labor-management efforts already underway, which are characterized by trust, open communication, and worker participation."

Final Words on the Need to Change

This chapter has discussed the need for changing the way we work. But more than that, it has attempted to stir some emotions about America's precarious position in the world marketplace. We need to concentrate on work improvement as a national strategy.

If you still aren't persuaded, ask yourself how you will answer your children when they ask 20 years from now, "You knew America had problems...why didn't you do something?"

Our workforce is talented, educated, knowledgeable, and creative, and can bring a wealth of innovative solutions to the problems that confront our organizations.

Participative management is a philosophy for bringing that talent, education, knowledge, and creativity to the forefront. Direct employee involvement in the decision-making process is the mechanism.

3 The Psychology of Employee Involvement

---

*Treat people as though they were what they ought to be and
you help them become what they are capable of being.*

—Goethe

No other aspect of employee involvement has so captivated me as what happens to the people exposed to it.

I've watched with immense satisfaction as front-liners go from skepticism to hope to optimism, from insecurity to confidence to pride as they become involved in activities that are meaningful in their organization.

I've also watched managers go through similar phases when they enter the process with willingness and patience.

Unfortunately, I've also witnessed the failures—the times when ego and insecurity have intruded, creating disharmony and blocking progress.

Understanding something about our behavior in the workplace can help clarify why employee involvement can work so well—or fail so miserably. The purpose of this chapter is to discuss those principles of human behavior that make employee involvement successful.

Needs and Motivation

To understand why employee involvement has such a stimulating effect on the human spirit, it helps to focus on those needs we have as human beings and what motivates us to higher levels of performance.

Maslow's Hierarchy of Needs

I hesitate to include this section because so many people, particularly in management, have been exposed to the concepts originated by psychologist Abraham Maslow. But there is such a direct correlation between Maslow's Hierarchy of Needs and employee involvement that I would be remiss if I omitted it. (If you're familiar with this concept, feel free to move down to the next subheading.)

Maslow theorized that the motivation to do something stems from our desire to satisfy some need. If we need something, we are motivated to take actions to get it. If we want it badly enough, we experience a certain amount of tension until we get it. So our **needs** create **tension**, and that tension causes us to take **action**.

Maslow went on to describe five levels of needs: Basic, Safety and Security, Belongingness, Ego-Status, and Self-Actualization. He said we tend to satisfy these needs in an ascending order from the simplest (Basic) to the most complex (Self-Actualization). Essentially, when we've achieved satisfaction on one level, we move to the next, and so on. This progression can be thought of as climbing the steps of a ladder.

The **Basic** level represents survival needs, such as food, clothing, shelter, and other necessities to sustain life.

The **Safety and Security** level represents the need for orderliness, protective rules, and general risk-avoidance. We tend to satisfy these needs by having an adequate salary, insurance policies, police and fire protection agencies, laws, social security, locks on doors, and burglar alarm systems.

When we've achieved satisfaction at the Safety and Security level, we move to the **Belongingness** level. At this level, we become less preoccupied with self, and begin to form interpersonal relationships. This level represents the need for family, friends, and group membership.

When we feel secure in these relationships, we attempt to gain special status within the group. This is the **Ego-Status** level. At this level, we desire recognition and awards. *Because satisfaction at this level is dependent on others to respond appropriately, it is the most difficult to achieve.*

If we've achieved relative satisfaction at the Ego-Status level, we move to **Self-Actualization**. At this level, we

41

become interested in personal growth, challenging ourselves to become more creative, demanding greater achievement of ourselves, and generally requiring ourselves to measure up to our own criteria of personal success. Self-Actualizing behaviors include taking risks, seeking autonomy, and developing freedom to act.

Let's look at this theory in practical terms.

In this country, most of us have no difficulty providing for survival and safety needs. We also tend to develop relationships easily—there are ample opportunities through family, religious affiliations, societies, sports, clubs, and work. Therefore, having satisfied these needs, many of us are looking to fulfill higher levels of needs, such as recognition and personal growth.

By contrast, the hungry or homeless could care less about recognition and personal growth. Their needs revolve around a daily struggle for food and shelter. They are clearly at the survival or basic level on Maslow's Hierarchy.

Needs Related to Work

A national poll was conducted by Business Week magazine and the Harris organization to find out what workers desire most in a job. The question asked was, "What two or three things do you want most in a job?"

The top four answers, in order of importance, were:
1. A good salary
2. Job security
3. Recognition for a job well done
4. A chance to use one's mind and abilities

The order of these responses correlates directly to Maslow's Hierarchy of Needs. The obvious conclusion: what workers **want** in a job is no different from what they **need** in their personal lives.

1. A good salary provides the Basic needs of food, clothing, and shelter.
2. Job security adds to the personal Safety and Security we seek in our lives.
3. Recognition for a job well done satisfies our Ego-Status needs.
4. A chance to use one's mind and abilities allows for personal growth and Self-Actualization.

Since World War II, most businesses have done an adequate job of providing good salaries and job security. In fact, surveys we've conducted show salary to be the <u>least</u> of the problems facing businesses. But few employers ever provide recognition for jobs well done, and rarely do they give workers the opportunity to stretch their minds and abilities.

Recognition

Some of the most deeply touching experiences I've had in employee involvement have been connected to the subject of recognition.

My first experience with the impact of recognition came on a construction project in St. Louis, Missouri. A crew of ironworkers had performed some outstanding work for us under very difficult conditions. The three-week job was completed in two weeks, well under budget, and without interrupting the client's assembly line production of an especially high quality product.

To show their appreciation, management sent letters to the homes of the crew members inviting them and their wives to a dinner in their honor at a local hotel.

The dinner was held on a Friday night and was a tremendous success. The following Monday morning, I was walking through the plant and came upon one of the crew members. He was a crusty old fellow whose skin was parched from years in the elements.

Normally he was loud and boisterous, but on this morning he was unusually quiet. Concerned, I asked him if anything was wrong. He said, "You know those letters you sent to our homes? When I got home that day, my wife was waiting for me at the door with the letter in her hands and tears in her eyes. She said to me, 'Jerry, you've been an ironworker for 30 years, and this is the first time anybody's thanked you for anything.'"

He was a changed man, and so was I. I couldn't believe that someone could work a lifetime and not be thanked for something!

This story was only the first of many. Since that time, I've often seen grown men and women overcome with emotion simply because someone took the time to recognize something they did well. It's an eye-opening experience—one that shakes you into realizing we just don't acknowledge, thank, recognize, or express appreciation enough.

When people are thanked or recognized, what happens is a "breaking through" of the Ego-Status barrier. There may also be a releasing of frustration when a good employee's work is finally noticed after years of trying. When employees finally succeed in achieving satisfaction on the Ego Status level, they can begin to seek higher levels of satisfaction.

Recognition is a powerful way to positively influence the behavior of people. When recognition is honest, fair, and frequent, people begin to realize that the organization greatly values the behavior being recognized. The workforce then tends to emulate the recognized behavior.

But when recognition is non-existent, biased, or unattainable, people become resentful. Particularly when recognition is non-existent in an organization, people get the message that good work performance is not valued there. The attitude becomes, "Why bother?" and performance sinks to some mediocre level.

Employee involvement provides recognition simply because someone is invited to participate in the management decision-making process. The message is "We recognize your talents, skills, creativity, and value to the organization." And that's recognition.

It also provides opportunities for front-liners to be more visible to management, thereby enhancing opportunities for further recognition.

Whatever the circumstance, a simple "thank you" is a powerful motivator used by successful managers. It's a way to let people know you don't take them for granted.

A Chance to Use Your Mind and Abilities

In the national poll referred to earlier, the fourth most important job characteristic desired by today's workers was "a chance to use one's mind and abilities." Forty or 50 years ago, simply having a job was a primary motivator, but today's workers have higher expectations of what work should be.

Money is no longer the driving force it once was. Studies by Yankelovich, Skelly and White have shown that 75% of Americans no longer find it acceptable to work at a boring job "as long as the pay is good"; and 78% say they would refuse to leave a job they like for one that pays more.[1] These are important messages for companies.

The rise in the standard of living of the average American has brought with it the expectation that work will always be there if you want it, and salaries will be sufficient to meet your basic needs.

What has not been guaranteed, however, is that the work will be challenging, meaningful, thought-provoking, and exciting.

Dr. Morris Massey would probably say that today's worker has been "value programmed" by television, seeing the heroes of *Mission Impossible* solve the world's problems in 60 minutes with four commercial breaks showing the good life. Television commercials tell us to "Live it up!" "Get all you can!" "Buy, buy!" and "Get it now!" Today's younger workers have had a lot and have experienced a lot. Is it any wonder they also expect a lot?

But the good side of this scenario is that today's workers have a strong desire to learn, explore, and create and a lot of energy that can be channeled to achieve greater innovation in our organizations. But we must <u>allow</u> that energy to be used.

In the summer of 1983, Hercules Corporation in Wilmington, Delaware, wanted to find out just how much energy there was in their organization. Though they had just moved into new headquarters a month earlier and there were the problems of summer vacations, the company launched a six-week crash effort to generate ideas to improve performance by 20%.[2]

Despite the difficulties inherent in such a crash effort, and though there had been no offer of incentives of any kind, the results were excellent. But more significantly, senior management was impressed with the high level of energy of the people.

In the words of Hercules Aerospace Company President, Edward Sheehy, "Hercules people respond to a challenge; that's just our nature. After we get over being mad about some jerk trying to press us beyond our limits, we say, 'OK, we'll do it.'"

The effort was accomplished in five weeks, producing 5000 suggestions for improvement. Most of these were implemented over the following two years.

A similar program involving 1600 employees of the Harleysville Insurance Companies of Harleysville, Pennsylvania, netted the company over $3.5 million in clear-cut savings in 12 weeks.[3]

Similar examples clearly show that there is a vast resource of energy and ideas lying untapped in our workforce. Management's role is to allow these ideas to surface, and, more than that, to encourage ideas for improvement as a way of life on the job.

When managers encourage input from employees, they play a large role in channeling tremendous energy back into the organization—energy that is critical to surviving in today's competitive climate.

Maslow's theory says that once we have satisfied our needs on one level, we tend to undergo tension related to achieving satisfaction on the next level. This **tension** will constantly be with us until we take some actions to satisfy the need.

Allowing employees to contribute their ideas to the company releases the tensions associated with the need for self-actualization, and provides an opportunity to "use one's mind and abilities."

What Happens Without Recognition and Self-Actualization

Since most organizations in our society do not provide opportunities for employee recognition and self-actualization, where does all that energy go?

As we are well aware, tension can lead to frustration which can lead to stress. And since stress is unpleasant and detrimental to our health, we tend to look for remedies to relieve it.

If we feel tension because of a need for recognition and self-actualization, we will take actions to obtain them. Since most waking hours are spent at work, our first inclination is to strive for recognition and self-actualization there.

But if the organization doesn't respond, and we see no hope of obtaining recognition and self-actualization there, we will look elsewhere. We may coach a Little League team, become active in professional or social organizations, run for public office, start a personal business, participate in charity work, and so on.

A manager at DuPont mentioned recently that senior management was surprised by the number of front-liners with occupations **outside the company**, a fact that came to light after they began implementing employee involvement concepts.

One can argue that employees should allocate time and energy to performing community service and other work of a volunteer nature. But the question becomes, what proportion of energy is being spent inside the organization versus outside?

Studies on work consistently show where the energy <u>isn't</u> going.[4] For example, studies by the Public Agenda Forum have shown that:

- Fewer than 1 out of every 4 jobholders say they are currently working at full potential.
- One-half say they do not put effort into their job over-and-above what is required to hold onto it.
- About 75% say they could be significantly more effective than they presently are.

What does this say about our workforce? What does it say about management?

Level of Effort

For just a minute, let your imagination take you back to when you first started working for your present company. (If that's too far back, then think of the last time you changed positions within the company.) Think of how you felt those first few days and weeks on the job.

Chances are you were excited, enthusiastic, industrious, and determined to show your bosses how good you were. Your motivation and resulting **level of effort** were high.

As time went on, however, that level of effort diminished some. Maybe you encountered some problems. Maybe you couldn't get the information you needed to do your job. Maybe your tools were defective or of poor quality. Maybe other people delayed your work. Maybe your commute to and from work began to get you down. Maybe nobody ever noticed that you were working your butt off for a little recognition. The list of "maybe's" could go on forever.

Whatever problems you were experiencing probably reduced your enthusiasm and, possibly, your level of effort.

The figure below is a simplified representation of level of effort. If the highest point on the graph is the maximum output you can give, and the low point the minimum level of output below which you would be fired, then the middle area becomes the area of **Discretionary Effort.** It is totally up to you (at your discretion) how much effort you will give. The area of discretionary effort can represent thousands of hours of lost production, missed opportunities for innovation, and poor customer service. The Public Agenda Forum studies mentioned earlier indicate most people are working somewhere well below the maximum.

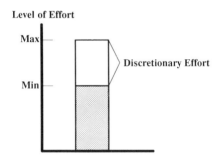

The question then becomes, how can we increase the motivation of workers to raise the level of this discretionary effort? What specific actions can we take to influence people to work nearer their potential?

One way is to eliminate or reduce some of the demotivators discussed before; for example, to provide better information, make available higher quality tools, reduce delays and disruptions to the work, provide recognition, and so forth. But how do we know what these demotivators are for individual employees? The only way to find out is to ask. These issues can be raised—as well as resolved—through employee involvement processes.

When managers create feedback mechanisms such as employee work improvement teams, open-dialogue staff meetings, or simply one-on-one discussions, these demotivators begin to surface.

Motivation and Job Enrichment

The subject of motivation would not be complete without discussing the concept of job enrichment proposed by psychologist Frederick Herzberg in the 1960s. Herzberg is generally considered the authority on the subject, and his concepts, tested repeatedly, have withstood the test of time.

The Theory

Herzberg proposed that a person's needs break down into two categories: hygiene factors and motivator factors.[5]

Hygiene factors are our biological needs, such as food, clothing, and shelter. (Note the similarity to Maslow's Basic level.) Herzberg says we have a built-in drive to **avoid pain** relative to these needs so we do what is necessary, such as work, to provide what we need. We simply don't want to be hungry, for example, so we do whatever we must to avoid it.

For our work setting, he refines the definition of hygiene factors as those things that make up our environment: salary, work conditions, supervision, relationship with co-workers, security, status, and company policy and administration.

Motivator factors include achievement, and through achievement, the ability to experience psychological growth. Motivator factors in the work setting include **achievement, recognition, the work itself, responsibility, and growth or advancement.** (Note the similarity with Maslow's Ego-Status and Self-Actualization levels.)

Herzberg's studies showed that motivators are the primary cause of job satisfaction, and hygiene factors the primary cause of dissatisfaction on the job.

Herzberg used the term **job enrichment** to describe how the motivator factors can be used to achieve higher levels of satisfaction with a job. The following list of principles was taken from his *Harvard Business Review* article of 1968 and reprinted in 1987. Meaningful job enrichment involves the following:

1. Removing some controls while retaining accountability (Responsibility and personal achievement).
2. Increasing the accountability of individuals for their own work (Responsibility and recognition).
3. Giving a person a complete natural unit of work (Responsibility, achievement, and recognition).
4. Granting additional authority to employees in their activity; job freedom (Responsibility, achievement, and recognition).
5. Making periodic reports directly available to the workers themselves rather than to supervisors (Internal recognition).
6. Introducing new and more difficult tasks not previously handled (Growth and learning).

7. Assigning individuals specific or specialized tasks, enabling them to become experts (Responsibility, growth, and advancement).

Herzberg distinguishes between job enrichment and job enlargement. Managers should note well the differences. Job enlargement changes the job structurally, yet has no lasting effect on motivation. Examples are:

1. Challenging the employee by increasing the amount of production expected. For example, from tightening 10,000 bolts a day to 20,000.

2. Adding another meaningless task to the existing one, usually some routine clerical activity.

3. Rotating the assignments of a number of jobs that need to be enriched. For example, washing dishes for a while, then washing silverware.

4. Removing the most difficult parts of the assignment in order to free the worker to accomplish more of the less challenging assignments.

If Herzberg's principles are valid, and the consensus is that they are, then how does employee involvement fit with this concept of motivation?

Employee Involvement and Job Enrichment

Does employee involvement relate to job enrichment, and therefore, serve as a motivator for employees? Let's look at some of the principles of job enrichment listed earlier and compare them with employee involvement concepts.

Increasing the accountability of individuals for their own work (Responsibility and recognition).

Without a doubt, there is a direct correlation with the concepts of employee involvement. In the case of quality circles, for example, members will identify and analyze specific problems in their group, and recommend solutions. Once their proposed solutions have been approved, they will usually be responsible for implementing the solutions, monitoring progress, and making adjustments where needed. The responsibility and resulting accountability for success is theirs.

Granting additional authority to employees in their activity; job freedom (Responsibility, achievement, and recognition).

Again we have a direct correlation with employee involvement. When employees are involved in problem-solving, for example, they must collect information about and analyze the causes of the problem. Management legitimizes the data collection process by allocating time for surveys, co-worker interviews, measurements, etc. It also provides time for the analysis of the data. Management has, in effect, granted new authority that hadn't previously existed.

The change in the role of the front-liner from someone who merely receives orders to someone responsible for problem-solving and innovation greatly enhances the worker's sense of achievement and recognition.

Introducing new and more difficult tasks not previously handled (Growth and learning).

Again there is a direct correlation with employee involvement. Using employee teams as an example, when people are removed from their normal work tasks for an hour a week to become involved in organization improvement, they are introduced to an aspect of running the company that is entirely new and different.

They learn problem-solving, team dynamics, and inter-personal skills. They experience the frustration of tackling difficult tasks previously designated as problems for management to solve, gaining new insights into the difficulty of managing an organization. They experience the fear of making a formal presentation to management, and then they feel the sense of pride and accomplishment when they've done it. They experience a tremendous growth in confidence as they are forced to go beyond the limitations they've placed on themselves.

Perhaps more than anything else, it's this aspect of personal growth that is so apparent through employee involvement. (Refer back to the stories in Chapter 1.)

Assigning individuals specific or specialized tasks, enabling them to become experts (Responsibility, growth, and advancement).

Again, there is a direct correlation with employee involvement. When employees are invited to participate in organization improvement by being given a specific task, they will naturally learn so much about that task that the term "expert" may apply.

A team of employees at Public Service Electric and Gas Company in New Jersey was given the problem of determining what kind of round-the-clock work schedule was best for plant operators "from a human factors point of view." Management was concerned that the shift schedule then in force might be contributing to operator errors.

The team researched the topic in depth and ultimately presented their proposed "best schedule" to management. In the course of doing their research, they became "experts" on the subject of how shift schedules affect human performance. Subsequently, they were called upon to make presentations to outside agencies and other electric utilities.

Although presentations to outside agencies can be considered somewhat unusual in employee involvement, the act of becoming "resident expert" on a subject is commonplace.

It should be clear that employee involvement concepts provide many valid opportunities for job enrichment and the resulting employee motivation. Especially in jobs where the work is repetitious and mundane, "mind-stimulating" employee involvement activities can provide workers with a challenge on the job and the opportunity for growth.

Self-Fulfilling Prophecy

The Theory of Self-Fulfilling Prophecy says that the expectation or belief that something will occur can actually cause it to occur.[6]

At the beginning of Chapter 1, I referred to a construction project in St. Louis, Missouri. The project lasted from 1981 to 1983, and, although we didn't realize it back then, it turned out to be a unique experience in influencing the behavior of people. I was the project engineer for the contractor, and the experience forever altered my beliefs about leadership and self-fulfilling prophecy.

I would, therefore, like to begin this section on Self-Fulfilling Prophecy by relating the history of this project. I believe this project is a unique and dramatic example of how the Theory of Self-Fulfilling Prophecy can work in the real world of business.

The Psychology of Employee Involvement

Background

Monsanto Company, headquartered in St. Louis, had been a producer of high-grade silicon for computer chips for many years. In 1980, their oldest facility, located just outside St. Louis, was in need of upgrading and repair.

At the same time, the Japanese had begun producing silicon "wafers," and had publicly proclaimed their plans to dominate this market. Since Japan had recently taken over other markets previously dominated by the United States, this was a real threat to U.S. suppliers like Monsanto.

Monsanto had a difficult decision to make. Should it streamline and modernize the St. Louis plant or build a new plant elsewhere? In St. Louis, Monsanto would have to deal with 15 to 20 separate construction trades unions on a project. Maybe, like many other owners in 1980, it should relocate the project to a non-union area.

Monsanto knew that the state of the technology of silicon wafer production was changing almost daily, and that there would be many design changes during the two-year project. Design changes result in tearing out completed work, and studies of construction workers have shown this to be the number one demotivator for good craftsworkers. Monsanto's Frank Hendrickson was aware of this fact and was concerned that construction productivity would be adversely affected.

After all economic factors were considered, however, Monsanto decided to upgrade the St. Louis plant rather than build down south. The modifications would result in construction costs of approximately $50 million.

The Seeds of Uniqueness

Frank Hendrickson was close to retirement. Under his guidance, Monsanto had been experimenting with worker motivation for several years. Although Hendrickson had been around a lot of construction projects in his years with the company, he had never before attempted to apply worker motivation concepts to the St. Louis unionized construction labor market.

Hendrickson's plan centered around creating a jobsite atmosphere where communication flowed freely, workers' ideas were encouraged, and people were thanked for their contributions. It was also included in the plan that the workers be made aware how important this job was to Monsanto. The threat from Japan was real.

To comprehend the absurdity of this plan, you have to understand the construction industry. In construction, work is usually short-term, so workers seldom develop any allegiance to their hiring contractor. Supervisors are usually autocratic and directive. A typical project may have up to 20 separate unions attempting to work together. Pressure to maintain established schedules is usually intense. And relationships between contractors and building trades leaders are not usually based on trust. It's hardly the ideal setting for creating an atmosphere of communication, innovation, and recognition.

In what I consider a stroke of genius, Mr. Hendrickson began looking for a contractor whose values would support his plan. Monsanto ultimately selected Fruin-Colnon Corporation of St. Louis for the job. Then, in a second stroke of genius, he chose to **personally interview and approve all contractor personnel who would run the job.**

As a "candidate" for project engineer, I, too, was interviewed. In my 10-year career in construction, nothing like this had ever happened to me before. I was asked crazy questions like, "How do you feel about soliciting ideas from workers?" and, "How can you let people know they're important on the job?" I wasn't asked a single technical question; all the questions were related to working with people.

Ultimately, and not surprisingly, the staff that emerged from this selection process was very "people-oriented." We all had similar views about the value of people and the contributions they could make to the success of the job. It was an unusual bunch.

The Dubious Task of Gaining Union Support

To gain union support for our plan, a presentation was made to the leaders of the 20 unions involved. Their reaction? They simply didn't believe what we were saying.

The president of the Building Trades Council said the plan just sounded like a typical management scheme to get their people to work harder. He wouldn't support it. The other local leaders agreed with his position.

If you think about it, this position shouldn't have surprised us. In our country, the relationship between labor and management has been so adversarial that for us to walk into a union hall and begin talking cooperation, teamwork, recognition, creativity, and communication would have had to seem a bit strange.

Our "fall-back" position: to get the union leaders to agree to not resist us if we went ahead with the program anyway, and we'd keep them informed of its progress. They agreed to that.

A Philosophy and a Self-Fulfilling Prophecy

One of the first things we did was to establish a **philosophy statement** for the job.

The philosophy statement was: *To create an atmosphere of open communication and active participation, so that we can better utilize the talents, skills, and inherent creativity of our people.*

Although we didn't realize it then, establishing the philosophy statement was probably the single most important step we took toward creating the atmosphere we wanted.

And it's only been in recent years that I've understood the connection between that philosophy statement and the concept of self-fulfilling prophecy.

What I understand better today is that our philosophy statement sent a strong message to the workers that they, indeed, had talents, skills, and creativity...a message that conveyed value and a sense of worth.

Contrast this to the stereotypical image of construction workers. Hardhat, hardnosed, hardheaded, dangerous, dirty, unproductive, and the list goes on. These are the labels we attach to other people we don't even know.

Over the next two years, there were about 300 craftsworkers on the project. During that time, we saw more "talent, skill, and creativity" than we ever thought possible.

Productivity

By 1981, construction productivity in America had been declining steadily for about 20 years. We decided that any good project should attempt to reverse this trend, so we suggested making "productivity" a theme for the job.

At that point, all the skeptics came out of the woodwork, both on the management side and the union side. Both groups said that workers didn't want to hear about productivity, and they'd just get angry if we talked to them about it.

We felt, however, that if we were going to base our job on mutual respect and trust, we would be getting off to a bad start by deceiving our workers. Many of the skeptics argued that we should talk about "performance" instead of the emotionally charged "productivity." But we held out for "productivity" and won. In fact, we developed a fancy slide orientation for all new workers, and the first slide said "PRODUCTIVITY" in big bold letters.

We found out that our skeptics were right, but for the wrong reasons. The workers did, in fact, get angry. But their anger stemmed from a pent-up frustration with the poor productivity in America. And, in their opinions, neither management nor their unions were doing enough to improve it. It was a helluva therapy session.

The Work Environment

The typical construction project is not the nicest of places to work. It has lots of dirt and mud...no place to eat...smelly, portable toilets. It's cold in winter, hot in summer.

We decided that if we were sincerely interested in improving productivity and creating an atmosphere that supported high performance, we would have to spend some money to improve the physical jobsite. Every attempt was made to pay attention to those items that typically served as demotivators for workers.

We built a nice temporary office building to house all owner, contractor, and subcontractor management people with equal offices for all. We brought in heated and air-conditioned trailers for each craft so the craftsworkers would have a place to eat, rest, and wash up. We opted for heated and air-conditioned toilet trailers (if you've ever been in a portable john at 0° or 100° F, you know the potential for demotivation). We also spread lots of gravel so people wouldn't have to slop around in the mud on rainy days.

To attract people to the job earlier in the morning (which reduces delays in starting work) we brought in a catering company to staff and supply a food trailer with hot and cold items.

Our company mandated that safety glasses be worn, so to increase the probability that people would wear them, our safety engineer chose the newest, most comfortable glasses on the market.

To create an atmosphere of teamwork among people represented by different contractors and unions, we decided to provide hardhats with an insignia unique to the job. First, we invited a few job stewards to pick out the most comfortable hardhat they could find, and bought enough for everyone on the job. We then assembled a committee of stewards and journeymen to develop a logo and motto for the job. (You'd think hardcore construction workers would scoff at such an idea, but they didn't. They had already seen that management was responding to some of their concerns, and credibility and trust were developing.)

The logo included hands clasped overhead in a sign of triumph, elements of the American flag, and the motto Craftsmen Helping America Maximize Productivity, or

C.H.A.M.P. The logo was first-class. It was subsequently used on many items in addition to the hardhats.

In a survey conducted at the end of the job, we asked the workers their opinions about their physical work environment.

- 96% of the people rated the facilities "Good" to "Excellent."
- 90% said the facilities were better than other jobs on which they had worked.
- 2 out of 3 workers said facilities influence their decision to stay with a job (turnover is a major problem in construction).
- 2 out of 3 workers said facilities influence their decision to come to work each day (absenteeism is also a problem).
- 3 out of 4 workers said the quality of facilities affect their ability to be productive.

We simply paid a lot of attention to environmental details in an attempt to eliminate all possible demotivators. Unknowingly, we were reinforcing the message that these people were of value to us. If you value something, you'll take care of it, pay more attention to it. By providing a comfortable work environment, our actions reinforced our words.

If you think that maybe we had an unusually good group of workers, the electrical steward informed me that the portable toilets on his last job were so poorly maintained and smelled so bad that the same craftsworkers had **burned them down.** At the end of our job, there was not a single mark of graffiti in our toilets.

People will respond in a manner consistent with the way they are being treated.

Are These Really Construction Workers?

Within a few weeks after starting the job, we began to notice some rather strange changes occurring in the workforce.

Our lead superintendent had a positive attitude toward all people, and treated everyone with the same expectation...that they were all people of value. But don't get the idea he was any "softy." He was a 260-pound ex-marine and boxer.

I had the office adjacent to his, and could hear when he talked to the craft supervisors on the radio. The first two weeks on the job, I was sure he was going to lose their respect because he was using a strange language on the radio. He used words like "please," "thank you," and "sir" to everyone he talked to. But to my amazement, within a few more weeks, his supervisors began using the same words, and not only with him, but also with each other. I'd never heard this type of language on a construction project before.

Besides this change in language, there were obvious behavior changes among the workers.

Not long after the craftsworkers moved into their trailers, one group of laborers installed curtains in theirs. Not to be outdone, the ironworkers then installed curtains in their trailer.

On a rainy day, you would see rows of boots lined up outside the trailers during lunch breaks. The workers simply wouldn't track mud into the nice facilities they had been given.

Our jobsite newsletter began to do interviews with craftsworkers about their personal lives away from the job. One had been a professional field hockey player with the St. Louis Steamers, several were skilled artists and woodcarvers, one was a former county judge running for state senate, one was a successful business executive who owned a specialty rug shop in an exclusive shopping mall, several had children who had received scholarships to college, one taught school in the evening, and so on.

The cumulative effect of this publicity was a dramatic change in management's perception of the typical construction craftsworker. The stereotype was crumbling.

As the Monsanto design engineers began to notice the talents and skills of the craftsworkers, they started to consult with them before finalizing their drawings. Since the project was in a "rush mode" most of the time, the engineers decided to minimize revisions by going out to the jobsite and talking "first-hand" to the workers who would be executing the job. In all my years as a construction engineer, I had never seen anything like it. Mutual respect was gaining a foothold.

To further enhance the spirit of teamwork, outside recreational activities were organized. Committees of craftsworkers and management staff organized and ran successful golf tournaments, softball tournaments, horseshoe tournaments, fishing tournaments, retirement luncheons, and more.

When you spend time with someone in a recreational setting, you begin to look at them in a different way. I teamed up with a sheetmetal supervisor for our bass fishing tournament. Since I knew nothing about bass fishing, I had to rely on his knowledge and experience to carry me through the day. We came to know and respect each other in a setting the jobsite didn't offer.

All these experiences led to a far different perception of the workers by others. Monsanto's executives began to comment on our workers, and our own executives were beginning to see these workers in a different light.

Communication

Communication was extensive, open, honest, and in some cases bold.

Most construction craftsworkers are typically brought onto a jobsite and immediately put to work. Many work for months without knowing the nature of the project.

As I mentioned earlier, we felt strongly that each worker must know the philosophy for the job and the reasons for it. We also felt that a frank discussion of productivity was in order. So we provided the workers with a two-hour orientation as soon as they reported for work from their union halls. This was a general orientation and included what the project was, why it was important to the owner, and what the workers needed to know about the worksite.

Two weeks later, after the craftsworkers had had a chance to settle in, we invited them back for a second orientation, focusing on productivity and the purpose of the C.H.A.M.P. Program. It was during these sessions that the workers vented their frustration with construction productivity in America.

Body language in these sessions always went from defensive (arms crossed and sitting back) to receptive, open, and involved (arms on table and sitting on the edge of the seat). More than once, a fist was slammed on the table to emphasize a point of frustration—for example, "Why would management (on other projects) direct work to be done one way when they knew well from years of experience it could be done better another way?"

Our response was, "We believe management is responsible for at least 80-90% of all productivity problems in our country." And we believed it.

But communication doesn't end when you've told the workforce what you <u>want</u> to tell them. It gets tougher. Let me explain.

Once, there was a jurisdiction dispute between the electricians and the pipefitters. The dispute was over who would install certain work that wasn't covered by their contracts. Typically, disputes like this are decided by the contractor. And, unfortunately, there is always a winner and a loser.

In this case, the project manager awarded the work to the pipefitters. The electricians—the losers—were angry. Actually, it was a particularly tough decision, and they were <u>very</u> angry.

Since I had established credibility with the workers, I was able to talk with some of the electricians and determine the source of their anger. They simply didn't understand how such a decision could be made against them.

I knew that the project manager, J. C. Ronquest, had worked hard on the decision and had made as fair a decision as possible. I went to him and asked if he would meet with all the electricians to explain how he had arrived at the decision.

At this point I have to say that this kind of meeting is unheard of. Most managers retreat to the safety of their offices until things die down rather than face an angry, hostile group of craftsworkers. But Ronquest was different. He was always as fair with people as anyone could be, and, therefore, not afraid to explain himself. He also knew that angry people are not productive people. He agreed to my request.

Ronquest held the meeting in a large conference room—just him, with all the electricians. After the meeting I asked some of the men how it went. They said, "Well, we still don't like the decision, but we now know how he made it. It's probably a fair decision considering all the information he had to make it."

Anger was defused, respect was gained, and a potentially demotivating situation was turned around, simply because a man had the courage to address a tough situation. Tough communication.

It has been my belief that the reason communication fails so frequently in organizations is that management doesn't recognize that workers can handle the tough stuff as well as the good stuff. We therefore tend to feed them Pablum.

After this incident, J. C. Ronquest wrote an article for our newsletter explaining in detail the entire process of resolving jurisdictional disputes. Another first.

Results

What we sought from the outset was productivity, and productivity was the result. Costs were running at or below the budget continuously until the project ended. Productivity

68

didn't come from a single idea or concept, but from a multitude of contributions from all hands.

For example, it had been suspected that some of the management systems we had implemented were slowing progress, so we conducted a formal Supervisor Delay Survey. Crew supervisors were asked to estimate every day for a week the number of hours their crews were delayed due to various circumstances.

The first results surprised us. We found that crews were being delayed an average of 20% because of various problems, such as:

- waiting for materials
- waiting for tools
- waiting for equipment
- design changes
- waiting for information
- overcrowded work areas

With the assistance of the supervisors, we began searching for ways to reduce these delays. Over the next six months, delays dropped from 20% to 14% to 9% to 7% and eventually bottomed out at about 5%. It was estimated that **the savings in work hours amounted to $12,000 a week.**

In the course of conducting these Supervisor Delay Surveys, we were surprised at the open and honest comments that were made. In evaluating delays for the day, one supervisor even blamed himself. He reported that he had lost time in obtaining materials his crew needed for a job, and went on to say, "If I had planned the work better and had given the warehouse ample lead time, I wouldn't have been delayed." This type of open confession is possible in an atmosphere of trust.

Ideas were in abundance. The individual contributions of all jobsite workers could fill a book.

One day, as I was passing a laborer chipping concrete off some forms, he pointed out to me that the hammer, chisel, and wire brush method was slow, and he had seen a tool that could do it faster. I immediately ordered a dozen, and personally delivered one to him when they arrived.

One of our cranes needed major repairs that an off-site repair shop estimated at $7000. Our mechanics said they could do it for less, even with the higher rates of pay on the jobsite. They planned and executed the work well and when all costs were tallied, the total tab was under $2000. More important, the crane was back in service a week sooner than expected.

We noticed also that as the job attitude improved, employee absenteeism and turnover dropped dramatically.

Absenteeism, which typically averages 10% in construction, leveled out at 2.5%, and turnover, which also averages 10%, leveled out at 1%.

One union business agent expressed his feelings about the excellent work attitude by pointing out to me one of his "problem children." It seemed this man was what he called "a four-day-a-week" worker. He just simply wouldn't show up more than that. "But in the last eight months on your job," the business agent said, "he hasn't missed a day!"

Harold Foley, President of the St. Louis Building and Construction Trades, put it this way: "You could not pry the men off the job!"

Another area of concern in construction is industrial safety. Insurance premiums in construction for workers compensation are high. But insurance companies will adjust the premiums in accordance with the company's safety record.

Fruin-Colnon's safety record was excellent, and so their insurance modifier was about half of the industry average. But even with this excellent modifier, our job's rate went even lower because our accident rate was about one-sixth the national average. Our insurance premiums were subsequently reduced accordingly.

The project's overall results were so favorable that Monsanto decided to extend the contract for another year, further upgrading the plant.

Publicity

As word spread around the construction industry about what we were doing, the job began to get media attention and a constant stream of visitors.

I found it strange at first that people would travel across the country to visit a construction job where the only difference was in the way people were treated. Treating people with common decency shouldn't be something special. We learn the "Golden Rule" as small children, but I guess as we grow up we think it doesn't apply to the business world.

Newspapers such as the *St. Louis Globe-Democrat* and the *Wall Street Journal* did articles on the project. Contractor organizations and professional societies did pieces as well. My favorites were those that appeared in the AFL-CIO publications, particularly the *St. Louis Labor Tribune*. These were truly positive articles that emphasized the good things that can happen when people work together and respect each other.

At the University of Texas Conference on Productivity Improvement, the C.H.A.M.P. program was heralded as "one of the two most successful productivity improvement programs in the country."

Even though the media represented different interests, the articles verified the program's effectiveness. Typically the reporters would try to find a crack in the statements coming from management. After talking with the staff, they would go onto the jobsite and talk with craftsworkers, apparently to see if workers' sentiments agreed with management's. They always did. The reporters would then become believers, and their articles reflected it. When a job is built on honesty and integrity, there's no need to color the facts. The results were there for everyone to see.

A Craftsman's Perspective

In September, 1982, one of the craftsworkers was moved to write an article for our newsletter. His name was Fred Parisi, a carpenter foreman for one of the subcontractors. His views echoed those of his peers and are reprinted here to emphasize the power of the self-fulfilling prophecy.

C.H.A.M.P. ...Looking Back One Year (A craftsman's point of view)

> When we started this program a year ago, a lot of questions were still unanswered by Labor.
>
> Management said to Labor, "We need your help, your input, in order to beat the imports and the economy."
>
> Upon two words the CHAMP Program was born: (1) Mutual Respect and (2) Communication.

Management made a commitment to be fair with people (Labor), provide decent restrooms and trailers and a place for hot meals. And, if Management made any mistakes, it would admit them. The CHAMP belt buckles, certificate awards, crew recognitions — all were the ideas of Management. So, you see, even before the CHAMP Program went into effect, a lot of people had to do their homework on Management's side. Because of the economy, car imports, rising interest rates, business (that is, Management) had to do something. They have! CHAMP was born.

Now Labor was very suspicious of this Trojan horse. Most of us, myself included, said "You're going to do all this for us? Yeah. Uh Huh. Well, what do we have to do for you in return?" Perhaps some of us still are suspicious. There is now another word that CHAMP should have in it; that word is Trust. We came into the CHAMP Program without trust. Management would have to prove itself with credibility in their actions and words. To help prove themselves, they formed a steering committee made up of 50% Labor (on site) and 50% Management (on site).

This committee would discuss worth and who was deserving of recognition by the Program. Safety—awareness of safety became a motivator. (no accidents meant two pairs of good boots at the end of the month. Winners selected from a drawing.)

Suggestions were and still are being asked for. The CHAMP Program here at Monsanto should mean two-way communication and mutual respect, confidence, and trust. The thing I admire here is Management's approach: first, try to solve the problem, second, attack the problem not the man.

After a year now with Monsanto and the CHAMP Program, I am very happy to say that I am part of it. I would wish to see the company I work for have such a program. Yes, there are those who have made fun of us, called us "chimps", "chumps", and other slurs. What can I say to these people? Go stuff it! You can't argue with anyone who can't reason out a motive. Management's motive and effort has been sincere, and so has Labor's.

Some of us now, a year later, might say "So what. Who cares? What did we prove?" Well, let me say to you this program works. The respect between trades is there; communication and respect with Management is there. We are the first on-site program like this anywhere. All of construction is looking at us to see how well we do, how well we respond, how well we participate. Believe me when I say there are large and small companies asking about us and what we do here. We are all very important to one another; let's not forget it. I could go on but won't. I applaud first my own peers. I recognize your cooperation and involvement. I applaud Management for the idea of the CHAMP

Program and giving it direction. I applaud Fruin-Colnon for walking the tightrope between Management and Labor which takes a great deal of experience. I'd like to say here and now, we are like family here.

CHAMP has reached its first plateau!

P.S. — Key words for Labor are involvement and doing your part. We just might change all of construction's ways for the better.

The Link to Self-Fulfilling Prophecy

So we return to Self-Fulfilling Prophecy. The Theory of Self-Fulfilling Prophecy says that *the expectation or belief that something will occur can actually cause it to occur.*

Many studies have been performed that validate this theory. In one well-known study, teachers were told that certain students were "exceptional" and "above average in I.Q." when in fact the students were "average." At the end of the school year, these students actually scored higher on tests to measure such traits.[7] Experiments of this type, performed repeatedly, have added significant evidence that self-fulfilling prophecy plays a major role in human behavior.

Why did the C.H.A.M.P. program work? Why was it so successful?

Because the project staff truly *believed* that its workforce was talented, skilled, and creative. They also believed that these workers were good people who would contribute to the success of the project if given the opportunity. Since the staff believed this, all their actions tended to support it. The workers then saw themselves as

75

having value, and therefore, responded in ways that could only benefit the job.

So let's return to employee involvement. Why is employee involvement so successful in organizations that nourish and support it?

Because the same kind of principle is at work. Rank and file workers are looked upon not as expendable tools, but as valuable resources and contributors to the organization. They are looked upon as people who have unique talents, skills, and creativity. And so they respond in kind.

Many organizations announce proudly, "Our people are our most important asset." Then they make a mockery of their words with actions to the contrary. They spend money to maintain equipment, but not to train employees. They set up systems to codify work procedures rather than encourage multiple-option and creativity. And perhaps, most degrading of all, they establish petty rules to control employee behavior—rules that govern: what minute to arrive at work, take a break, have lunch, and go home; how many days a year an employee can be sick; what constitutes a "death in the family;" and so on. Then they wonder why employees don't feel like the "most important asset" they say they are. Actions, indeed, speak louder than words.

As a CEO, or senior manager, or supervisor, ask yourself, "What do I think about the people working for me? Do I believe they have talents, skills, and creativity? Do I believe they are truly an asset to this organization? Do I trust them?" If you find yourself answering negatively to any of these questions, the people in your organization may be responding in kind.

People will respond in a manner consistent with the way they are being treated.

Self-Fulfilling Prophecy and the Subconscious Mind

What's behind the Theory of Self-Fulfilling Prophecy? Is there a pragmatic principle behind such a seemingly metaphysical concept? To understand how the theory works, we need to turn our attention to the subconscious mind.

We have only recently begun to realize how the subconscious mind affects the way we perform tasks.

Considerable work is being done with athletes to improve their skills through the use of mental techniques. An Olympic skier, for example, will use relaxation and meditation to calm the mind, and will then form a picture or vision of the perfect ski run. By repeating this technique over and over again, the skier can program directly to the subconscious mind the correct way of performing all the necessary moves. This technique works because **an image gets stored away exactly the same as an experience.**

Twenty years ago this concept was almost unheard of, but today these training techniques are common among professional and Olympic athletes. Studies have been performed that clearly show that there is significant improvement in athletic performance when this type of programming of the subconscious occurs.

Let's recall for a moment how the subconscious mind operates. As we discussed in Chapter 2, the mind has some 15 billion nerve cells, capable of storing an enormous amount of information. Virtually everything we see and learn in the course of our lives resides there. Once information is accepted and stored in the subconscious, it will affect our behavior from that point on.

A good example of programming the subconscious is the act of tying your shoelaces.[8] When you were a baby and your parents dressed you, you were too young to be aware of the act of tying your shoelaces. You were what they call an **unconscious incompetent.** You were unconscious of the act of tying your shoelaces, and you didn't know how to do it.

As a toddler, you became aware of someone tying your shoelaces, but you still didn't know how to do it. You were now a **conscious incompetent.** You knew your shoelaces were tied, but you still couldn't do it.

As you got older, your parents decided it was time you tied your own shoelaces. So they sat down with you and carefully demonstrated the necessary skills. You practiced and practiced until you could finally do it yourself. However, for a while you had to concentrate on every loop and tug. You were now a **conscious competent.** You had to consciously think about every step as you tied your shoelaces, but you could now do it.

As an adult, do you think about tying your shoelaces? Do you think consciously that this loop goes here and that loop goes there? Of course not. You tie your shoes automatically without thinking about it. You are now an **unconscious competent.** You can be simultaneously thinking about what you're having for breakfast and tying your shoelaces.

What allows you to do this is your subconscious mind. It has stored away the necessary steps in tying shoelaces and allows you to perform this act with great skill without consciously thinking about it.

The awesome power of the subconscious becomes clearer when we realize the large number of activities it controls at any one time.

For instance, look at the functioning of the subconscious when you drive a car. Most of the time, as an experienced driver, you don't think about the actions needed to drive a car, but the subconscious simultaneously:

- monitors appropriateness of speed
- checks centrifugal force on curves
- compensates for inclement weather
- determines rates of acceleration and deceleration
- determines the need for braking
- controls steering and alignment of the car on the road
- responds with the appropriate action in emergencies

Much of the time you perform these activities while you carry on a conversation with others, listen to the radio, daydream, and so forth.

In addition, the subconscious is regulating all of your biological functions as well! Your heartbeat, blood pressure, your five senses, body temperature, perspiration, and so forth. The subconscious mind is, indeed, a powerful tool.

It is, however, just a tool. It accepts anything we decide to put into it. And herein lies the potential problem. We can program negative thoughts and behaviors just as easily as we can program positive thoughts and behaviors.

Noted psychologist and philosopher Dr. Wayne Dyer cautions us about the off-handed comments we make in our everyday life.[9] For example:

"I'm nervous."

"I'm a lousy cook."

"I'm terrible at math."

"I'm tired."

Since the subconscious dutifully acts out what we put into it, this negative programming will probably become reality. One very interesting example of this negative programming concerned the death of famous tightrope walker Karl Wallenda.

As recounted in the book *Leaders* by Warren Bennis and Burt Nanus, "Shortly after Wallenda fell to his death in 1978 (traversing a 75-foot high wire in downtown San Juan, Puerto Rico), his wife, also an aerialist, discussed that fateful San Juan walk, 'perhaps his most dangerous.' She recalled: 'All Karl thought about for three straight months prior to it was **falling**. It was the first time he'd ever thought about that, and it seemed to me that he put all his energies into **not falling rather than walking** the tightrope, making certain that the guy wires were secure, something he had never even thought of doing before.'"[10]

Although it appears to be a subtle difference, the mind programs "not falling" differently from "walking." The mind sees falling rather than walking, and in the case of Karl Wallenda, fulfilled what it was programmed to do.

How does this relate to business? Just as we had unknowingly sent a message of worth to our construction workers (remember the philosophy statement, "...so that we can better utilize the **talents, skills, and inherent creativity** of our people"), employee involvement sends a message of worth to all employees. The message gets programmed that they have value, knowledge, talent, skills, and creativity, and the subconscious begins to act on a new set of beliefs.

Reread the examples at the beginning of Chapter 1. Reread the story of the Monsanto project in this chapter. Earl Nightingale once said that **people become what they**

think about all day long. Although this concept has been around most of this century, it's only in the last few years that its meaning has been fully understood and accepted. We see examples of this over and over again in employee involvement.

What concerns me are the surveys that report that executives and managers believe that workers today are lazy, that they don't care about their jobs, and that they generally lack a good work ethic.

If management truly believes that, then that's the message they'll be sending to their employees...and that's the way their employees will respond. What kinds of messages are you sending to your organization?

Effects of Frustration

No discussion of the psychology of employee involvement would be complete without a discussion of frustration as it exists in the workplace. Several years ago I read Frederick Herzberg's *Management of Hostility* and was overwhelmed by its relevance to employee involvement.[11] It seemed to answer some of the questions that had nagged me for many years regarding frustration, and why employee involvement seems to be providing a valuable outlet.

Herzberg says, "Any time you manage people you have to frustrate them—it's the name of the game, and no amount of agonizing is going to negate this reality. However, the danger to the organization lies in extending this tacit contract to include the statement, 'When I do frustrate you, don't you dare express your hostility to me—I am the boss. Go home and kick your dog, go join a kook organization, or go eat your heart out—that is, turn the hostility back on yourself.'"

When employees are frustrated by the organization or the manager, there's usually no way of expressing this frustration directly. If the employees tell their bosses, "Go to Hell!" they stand the chance of being fired, so they don't vent their frustration (hostility) on its source.

Instead, the employees either displace the hostility or internalize it. If they **displace** it, they take it out on someone else; if they **internalize** it, they direct it at themselves.

Let's take an employee who has been frustrated by his boss, but can't respond to him directly. The man goes home, and if supper is a little late, he screams and yells at his wife. (More than once in my work in employee involvement I've had a spouse comment on a positive change of behavior.)

Herzberg says that the amount of hostility released in displacement is many times greater than the source of the frustration. So having hamburger for supper rather than steak becomes the basis for a major tirade.

I recently went to an NHL hockey game in Philadelphia and was shocked when the entire audience cheered in glee as two of the players beat each other's brains out. Could the audience be demonstrating displaced hostility?

From an organization's point of view, this may not seem serious...who cares if people cheer as hockey players beat each other up? For the organization, the problems begin when employees turn their frustration toward the organization itself. D. L. "Dutch" Landen, who spent 25 years with General Motors, once said that a worker who puts a wrench in the fender of a new car is **motivated** to do it. What motivated the employee to sabotage the car was frustration leading to hostility...a hostile action taken against the company itself!

Once when I was in a restaurant, a woman came running up to me with tears streaming down her face. Before initiating an employee involvement effort in her company, we took a survey of employee attitudes about the organization. Then we published the results in the company's newsletter. She explained that we had published all the problems the employees in her group had talked about for years, but were afraid to tell anyone in management about for fear of reprisal. Publishing the survey results had lifted the burden of years of frustration.

Herzberg goes on to say, "If you cannot express your hostility directly at the person who is frustrating you and you cannot displace your hostility to another person, and all other avenues for expression of your hostility are blocked, where can the hostility go? Only one direction is possible: the hostility must be directed back into yourself. Psychologists call this **internalization**.

"When hostility is directed toward oneself, it leads to depression, self-hate, self degradation and, ultimately, psychological suicide. If we look around us in industry today, we can see employees who no longer have any interest in what they do, who merely respond as automatons on their jobs, and who have indeed been forced to commit psychological suicide. In this final solution for the individual lies a great hidden cost for the organization."

What kind of manager could accept a direct expression of hostility without becoming upset? Herzberg says, "It will be the **manager of competence**. Contrariwise, it will be the **manager of slogans** who will not be able to tolerate the hostility of his subordinates. If you attack a manager of competence, he will accept it as a challenge, but if you challenge a manager of slogans, he will consider it to be a personal attack. The manager of competence is not destroyed by hostility, but the manager of slogans finds hostility dismantling his smoke screen and cannot withstand the challenges to his ability."

So what does a manager of slogans do to keep from being discovered? Herzberg says the manager of slogans comes back with counterhostility, or the familiar "backlash." This is what the woman in the restaurant was afraid of, and why she never vented her frustrations to management.

Herzberg summarizes his point by stating, "The issue facing management is to avoid forcing the employee to displace or internalize hostility and to accept and handle the direct expression of hostility."

In my years of working in employee involvement, one of the most gratifying aspects of the work has been watching the levels of frustration diminish. As employees begin to discuss and resolve problems that have frustrated them for years, a certain calmness enters their personalities, as though a heavy weight has been lifted from their shoulders. Their behavior becomes more relaxed, and energy levels rise. Energy is focused on improving the organization rather than badmouthing management. The change is dramatic.

Final Words on the Psychology of EI

When I started working in employee involvement, I was completely unaware of the psychological implications. But then we began to observe the behavior changes of the workers, and began to hear comments from their friends and spouses. We were experiencing a dramatic and powerful change that extended beyond the confines of the workplace. We were dealing with a concept that was affecting the whole person.

It was then, and only then, that we realized how tragic it is when a management system doesn't understand the need for recognition, self-actualization, and job enrichment...and doesn't understand that how we treat people will largely determine how they respond and perform.

The information in this chapter is important. But the real challenge is to remove it from the textbooks and apply it in our daily lives.

4 Resistance

*Any change, even a change for the better, is always
accompanied by drawbacks and discomforts.*

—Arnold Bennett

Resistance to employee involvement is real. Since 1970, when the concept of employee involvement was first introduced in America, resistance has caused the failure of many employee involvement efforts. It's puzzling that a concept that produces both tangible benefits for the organization and a great deal of satisfaction for the workforce creates so much resistance.

Since we tend to resist anything new and unfamiliar to us, initial resistance to employee involvement is normal. But the kind of resistance that causes outright failure of programs is much more serious. It's a deeply embedded resistance that many times is not even understood by the resisting person.

Although there is some resistance in the workforce and union leadership, the primary concern is management.

In the upcoming sections, we'll look at the sources and causes of resistance and what can be done to overcome it.

Sources of Resistance

Resistance to employee involvement comes from the three primary areas of an organization:

- workforce
- unions
- management

Workforce

An organization's front-liners experience some resistance at the outset. They simply don't believe management is serious, and, therefore, feel this is just another program that will come and go. This skepticism is especially significant among older members of the workforce who have indeed seen many programs come and go.

Organizations implementing employee involvement concepts typically go through a "Credibility Phase" for the first year or two of the program. Until the workers actually see it working, they have trouble believing in it.

Unions

In an organization whose workers are represented by a union, resistance by the union leadership is an outgrowth of the adversarial relationship unions have historically had with management.

The union naturally questions management's motives for implementing an employee involvement effort. Is management trying to get the employees to work harder? Is management trying to drive a wedge between the members and the leadership? Is management trying to destroy the union? It's natural for any union leader to ask these questions when first confronted with the notion of employee involvement.

I was once talking with the president of an Independent Steel Workers Union about his company's successful employee involvement effort. As the union's president, he had been involved with the effort from the beginning and was an avid supporter.

He told me a story of another company that came to see their program. Included in the entourage was his union counterpart. Uncomfortable with what he was seeing, the other president asked, "If this stuff works so well, why do they need a union?" He answered, "If this stuff works so well, why do they need management?"

This kind of dialogue reveals the concern of union leaders for the future of their unions.

Resistance by union leaders results when they are not involved with the implementation from the outset.

Florida Power and Light Company, for example, runs what is considered one of the most successful employee involvement efforts in the country today. By their own admission, however, their beginning was a bit rocky. FP&L initially kicked off their Quality Improvement Program without inviting the union leadership to participate. The leadership resisted, and the start of their program suffered.

A Delaware Valley chemical company has been experiencing ongoing difficulty with an employee involvement program in one of their plants. The company tried to implement the program from the top down without involving the local union leadership, and resistance took the form of outright withdrawal from the effort. The union's leadership has conducted meetings and invited speakers opposed to employee involvement in an attempt to dissuade their members from participating.

But these leaders are running a great risk in resisting the implementation of employee involvement. Employees today are greatly concerned about the future of America and the future of their organizations, and are looking for ways to contribute. We consistently see new union leaders voted into office who represent the values of high productivity and quality work.

Union leaders at the national level are working with management and the federal government on councils to improve the workplace. For example, the Economic Policy Council Productivity Panel includes several well-known and highly respected union leaders:

- John Carroll, Executive Vice President, Communications Workers of America
- Frank D. Martino, President, International Chemical Workers Union
- Charles H. Pillard, International President, International Brotherhood of Electrical Workers
- Jack Sheinkman, Secretary-Treasurer, Amalgamated Clothing and Textile Workers Union
- Glenn E. Watts, President, Communications Workers of America

In a report issued following a two-year study on employee involvement, this panel concluded:

"By involving personnel at all levels of an enterprise in problem-solving and decision making, by enriching the working lives of employees, by helping resolve personal concerns that affect their job performance, and by creating a climate in which people can achieve job satisfaction through directing their creativity and talents toward improving their work and their work environment, **worker participation programs can provide a foundation for sustained productivity growth.**"[1]

In a radical change of direction in 1985, the AFL-CIO Executive Council decided to shift their emphasis from winning wage and benefit increases to winning dignity and individual freedom for their members. They felt that workers today are more interested in having a say in their work than they are in pay scales and benefit packages.[2]

So the message is clear from the national leadership, and local union officials must recognize and support the move toward worker participation, or face serious consequences from either their national leaders or by the ballot of their members.

Management

Ask someone how their employee involvement effort is going and the typical response is, "It's OK, but it sure could work better if management would pay more attention to it," or "We just can't get our management interested."

The Association for Quality and Participation periodically dedicates whole issues of its journal to the subject of management support, and their conferences draw large numbers of participants to sessions on the same subject.

The Association's chapter in southeastern Pennsylvania recently surveyed their membership to find out what topics to include in their own local conference. Not surprisingly, the number one topic again was management support.

A 1982 study conducted by Robert Cole and Dennis Tachiki of 218 early adopters of Quality Circles concluded, "A great majority of our respondents report middle management resistance (79%) and the lack of top management support (71%) as **the top two factors** hindering the spread of quality circles within their firms."[3]

I know of an employee involvement effort that recently died of neglect. The first two years of the program returned an estimated $2 million to the organization, or a return on investment of about 6 to 1. But management placed the effort low on its priority list, and it died a slow but certain death.

In any organization, management sets the tone for the operation of the whole organization. Management determines policies and priorities. Management creates the work atmosphere and its characteristics: trusting, respectful, positive, comfortable, innovative, quality-conscious, productive, ethical.

Essentially, the way management **thinks** becomes the character of the organization. Management consultant Jeff Beardsley puts it this way: "Replace the bottom half of the organization with a new set of workers and what changes in the organization? Nothing. But replace the top half of the organization with management that thinks differently, and instantaneously the organization changes."[4]

Managers have the power to influence the behavior of an organization in a thousand different ways. According to Tom Peters, front-liners watch managers constantly for signals of how to behave. "In the course of the average day," he says, "every single manager is served up a thousand opportunities to make his interests known. The little penned notes on the corner of a memo, seating arrangements at a meeting, the little words dropped on the side at a meeting, the order in which he visits people when he goes out to the field, the places he decides to visit first in the field. And every single one of those things are interpreted endlessly, hour after hour by every single person in the organization."[5]

The same signals are sent to employees regarding employee involvement. Do the managers involve people in decisions that will affect them? Do they talk with team leaders and members regarding their progress? Do they occasionally visit quality circle or improvement team meetings to keep in touch with their progress? All too often the answer is no.

One excellent employee involvement team we worked with had been in existence for about a year and a half. During the team's first few months of work, their manager visited them three or four times, reinforcing the need for their work. During the last year of their existence, however, the manager totally neglected the team, and despite requests from the team's facilitator, would not come to their meetings. Regardless of his intent, the message to the team was that their work was no longer important to him. At the completion of their last project, they disbanded. Incredibly, the company estimated that one of the team's projects would return $900,000 to the organization over the next five years.

Management resistance to employee involvement is hard to address because it's deeply rooted in basic psychological principles, and, therefore, may be manifested in subtle ways. We'll look at these psychological principles later.

Causes of Resistance in Management

Resistance in an individual manager may result from one specific cause, but it's more likely to be caused by a combination of factors, such as:

- Insecurity
- Personal Values
- Ego
- Management Training
- Managers Not "High Touch"
- Managers Left Out

Insecurity

In varying degrees, we are all insecure; unfortunately, we are taught to be insecure early in life. But the extent to which our insecurity affects our behavior is largely determined by how insecure we are. We all know people who exude "self-confidence," and we all know people who tremble with insecurity. The degree of insecurity varies widely.

Insecurity in supervisors or managers is a significant problem when it manifests itself in their behavior with subordinates. Historically, though, this insecurity has remained in check because managers have typically been in control of the flow of information. Participatory management concepts, by their very nature, bring latent insecurity to the surface.

When employee involvement concepts are implemented, there is intense scrutiny of group operations and problems. Employee involvement legitimizes opening up the organization, bringing problems to the surface, and resolving them.

Since front-liners are in a good position to see problems in the work, they tend to expose a great number of problems.

Picture a new employee involvement team that has just been formed in a department. Maybe the supervisor is relatively secure, and even supports the concept of participative management.

The team sits down for its first meeting and begins brainstorming problems in the department. The brainstorming—an effective tool for generating ideas—results in a list of 70 or 80 or 90 problems. The supervisor looks at the list and is horrified, having expected 10 or 15 items—not 90!

Upon seeing his team's list, one manager we know lamented, "What if my manager sees this list? He's going to wonder what I'm doing down here!"

This kind of experience is guaranteed to bring some insecurity to the surface. It's perfectly normal. But if there's too much insecurity, the supervisor or manager will tend to resist the employee involvement effort.

Now let's look at insecurity from a broader perspective. The trend today is to think our management ranks are bloated and need to be reduced.

In the videotape *In Search of Excellence* being used by many companies, Dana Corporation Chairman Jerry Mitchell proudly tells us how **reducing management layers from 14 to 5** helped the company grow from a $1 billion to a $4 billion organization.[6] When I've shown this tape myself, I've seen more than one supervisor squirm in their seats.

Companies are not only cutting out layers of management voluntarily. It has been estimated that in the period 1983 through 1988, 1.5 million middle and upper-level managers will have been displaced from major corporations as a result of cutbacks, takeovers, mergers, and business failures.[7]

The irony is that most people, including managers, will agree that we're top-heavy in our organizations. But what is never discussed is what we will do with all those managers; and without such a discussion, they will revert back to the lower levels of Maslow's Hierarchy to safety and security. When we find our livelihood threatened, we tend to take actions to protect it.

A natural step toward reducing management ranks is creating a more competent workforce. Employee involvement, which teaches front-liners management techniques, problem-solving techniques, and interpersonal skills, may be perceived as the method by which we will ultimately reduce management layers.

In a survey of first-line supervisors conducted by Janice Klein of the Harvard Business School, "Nearly three-fourths (72%) of the first-line managers surveyed viewed employee involvement as being good for the company, and more than half (60%) felt it was good for employees, but less than one-third (31%) viewed it as being beneficial for themselves."[8]

Needless to say, employee involvement programs put insecure managers or supervisors in an awkward position. If they support the effort, they may be ultimately eliminating their own jobs. So we begin to see them—mostly subtly, but sometimes blatantly—resisting.

In my work as a team facilitator once, I witnessed an example of sabotage that confirmed my feelings about insecurity in management.

The general manager of an organization's quality assurance department formed a new team. A lower level manager whose subordinates became the team members was somewhat uncomfortable with the new team. After the team's first meeting, he called in one of the younger members for a three-hour grilling, demanding to know what had transpired at the meeting and the names of members who had made various statements and proposals. When I found out about the interrogation, I explained to the manager that it was inappropriate for him to ask for names—we tell the teams that it's OK to discuss subject content, but not who said what. I also invited him to attend the meetings; he declined.

After several more meetings, team members were beginning to get nervous about their participation on the team. The manager's actions were making everyone uncomfortable. In a final desperate gesture to subvert the team, he began spreading untruths that he attributed to me about the team. He was attempting to drive a wedge between the members and me, their facilitator.

I ultimately had several conversations with the manager to try to allay his fears about the team's work, but I was dealing with an extreme case of insecurity. It took many more months before the team reached a reasonable level of productivity.

Most insecurity is not acted out as overtly as this. Most of the time it appears as what I call "subtle sabotage." Maybe the supervisors don't attend any of the team's meetings, or maybe they make it difficult for a member to attend. Maybe they increase the work load of the members and then make them feel guilty when it's time for their meeting. Maybe there's a subtle put-down of the team's ideas and work. Maybe they approve team recommendations, then drag their feet on implementation. Subtle sabotage takes many forms, and has the cumulative effect of demoralizing the team.

Much of the time, a demoralized team will disband, leaving a bad taste in everyone's mouth about employee involvement.

The organization loses, but the supervisor loses more. Those participating on an improvement team see the potential and the obvious benefits to the organization. The manager or supervisor who doesn't support the effort loses credibility and respect rapidly.

Insecurity with employee involvement is also experienced by those whose functional responsibilities may be threatened by its implementation.

For example, labor relations departments have classically been the primary contacts with union personnel. In some organizations, all communication with the union is the exclusive domain of the labor relations department.

Employee involvement creates many opportunities for union personnel to interact directly with their non-union counterparts in management, thereby eliminating the traditional communication path through labor relations. Some labor relations representatives see this as a threat to, and subsequent weakening of, their authority and, therefore, tend to resist the implementation.

Although no studies have been done yet on the relationship between insecurity in management and employee involvement, we feel that it's a primary cause of resistance to the concepts.

Personal Values

As we discussed earlier, arguments and misunderstandings over employee involvement stem from conflicting personal value systems.

98

Our value systems are those beliefs we hold that help us (and more so, <u>cause</u> us) to make judgments about the world around us. Our value systems are formed early in life, but all of our experiences in life shape our values in some way.

Many people in management positions today developed their value systems in the years prior to World War II. For the most part, those were years of some deprivation, and you were grateful if you simply had a job.

Some of these managers are tied strongly to these values. They have a difficult time understanding a younger work-force whose value systems were shaped by post-war prosperity...value systems in which work is regarded as a right rather than a privilege.

For some managers, then, their value systems are the source of resistance. They think employee involvement means "coddling workers" and are contemptuous of any attempts to do so.

One manager I worked with refused to attend any employee team meetings, and resisted requests to become involved in supporting the effort. He simply didn't feel that this sort of "coddling" was appropriate. He held onto this belief until his retirement.

Understanding how a value system contributes to a person's behavior is essential in dealing with the problems that will inevitably arise during the implementation of employee involvement concepts.

Ego

Becoming a supervisor or manager for the first time is exciting. Usually, the person has worked hard and excelled. The promotion to supervisor is the organization's way of recognizing the person's talents and previous success in the job.

In their roles, supervisors and managers enjoy certain privileges. Most of the time (but not in all cases) they:

- have their own offices
- don't perform "grunt" work
- are privy to new information
- attend special meetings
- receive special training
- are paid more
- have special benefits

And some of the time (more in the past than today as our attitudes are changing about these), they have special parking places, special dining rooms, and special rest rooms.

These special privileges tend to set up a class system between the "special" people and the "not so special" people. I don't mean to imply that all supervisors and managers walk around strutting; more likely, it's a subtle feeling that is ever-present in their subconscious.

Some supervisors and managers feel omnipotent, or feel that within their groups, they possess superior knowledge of the group's work. They consequently see themselves as the providers of answers to any and all questions.

When the organization begins changing to a more participative style of management, some supervisors and managers see this as an encroachment on their exclusive territory. They are the leaders, the ones with the answers, and they resent having to involve subordinates in something that is clearly their own responsibility.

A supervisor we know was once offended by his work improvement team because they asked him to share his goals and objectives with the department. He had been intending to share them all along, but because the team asked for them, he resisted. They were the initiators, not him. Sharing his goals and objectives would now look like a triumph for the team, rather than his own bright idea and initiative.

Ego manifests itself in other ways. Employee ideas, and particularly employee team presentations, can threaten managers who have large egos.

A manager we know was highly upset by a team's presentation to improve the method by which tools on a construction site were issued. It seems the manager was responsible for tool issuance, and was insulted that the team felt improvements could be made. He was so upset, in fact, that he went straight to the site manager's office and demanded that the entire employee involvement program be discontinued.

The extent to which ego affects how supervisors and managers relate to employee involvement programs has not been scientifically studied. However, our past conditioning and training regarding the role of management, and the class system created by the special privileges contribute to the development of ego type problems.

Management Training

At the Weirton Steel Corporation in Weirton, West Virginia, I was impressed by a talk given by Alan Gould, head of Employee Participation Groups, at a training session for group members. Gould reviewed the evolution of management theory in this country.

In the late 1700s, we had many specialized trades to produce most of the products and services we needed. We had pewterers, candle makers, blacksmiths, clothiers, leather workers, glass makers, gunsmiths, and so forth. These craftsworkers typically constructed the entire piece; in the case of the gunsmith, it was literally "lock, stock, and barrel."

In 1798, the government feared there would be war with France and needed to equip an army rapidly with 10,000 muskets. But the production of muskets through gunsmiths was a slow process, too slow to meet this demand.

So the government awarded a contract to Eli Whitney to produce the muskets. Using a system of molds and jigs, Whitney made it possible for an average worker to file and shape a part until it fit the pattern and then send it to another worker for assembly. By having workers create only one part of the musket over and over, Whitney was able to increase production dramatically and ultimately satisfy the government's requirement for arms.

For this achievement, Eli Whitney is considered the father of the System of Mass Production in our country.

This system had obvious benefits. It brought more people into the workforce at a time when the country was growing. It dramatically increased methods of production, resulting in lower, more affordable prices.

These benefits overshadowed a negative side-effect that has gone virtually unnoticed until this century. It used to be that the worker had the challenging task of producing an entire piece; with the advent of mass production, the worker had a much smaller task...a task that's repeated over and over...a task that requires little thinking. In effect, **mass pro-**

duction began to draw the worker away from the thinking process of the job.

About a hundred years later, Henry Ford carried this process one step further with the concept of the moving assembly line. Now the worker had only to stand in one location as the work moved by. In effect, the worker became part of the machinery, and the worker was drawn even further away from the thinking process of the job.

Frederick Taylor carried this another step and actually began to define the roles of management and labor.

Taylor was a brilliant mechanical engineer whose work at the turn of the century has significantly influenced management thinking to the present. Taylor was totally occupied with concepts that would increase production in manufacturing. Although some of his work dealt with employee incentives and morale, his work on time studies and organizing and streamlining the production flow has received the most attention. Taylor taught managers to analyze the work flow and devise methods of improving it. His principles of "Scientific Management" became widely accepted.

Management was quick to adopt these steps for improving production because relationships with labor were generally poor in the late 1800s. Management was continuously looking for methods of dealing with the "labor problem," and Taylor's scientific approach permitted them to deal with work flow procedures and equipment improvements rather than the more complex issues of employee commitment and morale.

Taylor believed that it was the "experts" who solved problems in organizations. And the culmination of his work was a philosophy that clearly defined management's role as the "thinker" and labor's role as the "doer"; that is, management does the thinking, and labor does what management says.

Although this approach is inappropriate in today's society, most of the work in our country is still performed according to this philosophy.

We have trained our managers well that they are responsible for the ideas and creative thinking in the organization, and when we ask them to implement employee involvement concepts, we're trying to undo that training. In these rapidly changing times, we've recognized the need to tap the resource of knowledge in the workforce. We're now saying to our managers, "Go out and ask your people for ideas." We've spent the last 70 years of this century operating one way, and now we're asking management to change by 180°. Is it any wonder some managers are confused?

A 1987 article in *The Philadelphia Inquirer* confirms that this archaic management training still continues. In their article on Weirton Steel, they talked with Jim Griffith, a 36-year-old supervisor in the tin mill. As a supervisor, Griffith said he had to learn to change the way he related to the men who worked for him. "It used to be that you'd go and say, 'Do this,' and they'd say, 'Why?' and you'd say, 'Because I said so.'"[9]

Resistance stems from confusion and misunderstanding, and it will take a concerted effort to unfreeze the old styles and incorporate the new.

Managers Not "High Touch"

By the very nature of employee involvement, supervisors and managers find themselves interacting more closely with their subordinates. Problem-solving creates the need for more information, and, consequently, more intensive dialogue within groups. Some in supervisory positions are uncomfortable with this closer interaction, and so resist. In their work on management personalities, Raymond E. Alie and L.M. Church have raised some interesting questions about the characteristics of management today. In a 1986 study of 82 middle managers, 74 "demonstrated no inclination to take the feelings or values of others into account when problem solving or making decisions. Accordingly, it can be argued that managers who exhibit little or no **feeling** orientation may not be prime candidates for participative management programs, such as quality circles, quality-of-work, or MBO."[10]

Our system of promotions tends to reward those who are successful at task accomplishment. We highly value someone who has the personal ability to accomplish something. We also value initiative, technical competence, organizational ability, ability to plan, ability to coordinate, and fiscal responsibility. These are all the traits of a task-oriented person, and these are the traits that take precedence when we evaluate someone for promotion to supervisory positions.

But history has shown (supported by studies of group dynamics) that the most productive leaders are those who have a balance of task-orientation and **group building and maintenance traits.**

Group building and maintenance traits include encouraging, harmonizing, compromising, rewarding, and communicating, to name a few. They are traits that tend to strengthen the group as a group, fostering trust, mutual respect, harmony, dedication, and cohesiveness.

For some reason, we have omitted ability in these areas from our criteria for promoting supervisors and managers. And not surprisingly, the number one concern of employees at all levels is communication.

Many surveys on employee attitudes verify this concern, but some of the best are the ongoing surveys of Opinion Research Corporation of Princeton, New Jersey. In summarizing their findings, they have found that "Perhaps the most important finding to emerge from this study of trends in employee attitudes toward internal corporate communications is the strong evidence that top management is becoming more isolated from its employees and less responsive to their concerns. There is every indication that employees believe that management has cut back on the flow of information to them and that their companies have become more hierarchical, i.e., run in a more autocratic fashion today than they were in the late Seventies."

They go on to say that "an increasing majority of employees in almost all groups say that their companies are losing **touch** with individual employees."[11]

Management consultant Tom Peters believes, "The single most significant managerial productivity problem in the United States of America is managers who are **out of touch** with their people and out of touch with their customers."[12] And this at a time when the experts say we need more of the human element brought into our workplace!

In his best seller *Megatrends*, John Naisbett concludes, "Whenever institutions introduce new technology to customers or employees, they should build in a "high-touch" component; if they don't, people will try to create their own or reject the new technology. That may account for the public's resistance to automation and electronic accounting."[13]

A concept that is gaining popularity as we have recognized the need for more interaction is MBWA, or Management By Wandering Around (we'll talk more about MBWA in a later chapter). For managers to be well-informed about the performance in their organizations or the needs and perceptions of their customers, we've learned that they must interact with co-workers and customers.

But watch what happens when some managers are asked to walk among their subordinates. The situation gets very awkward. We just haven't stressed these interpersonal skills in our management training or made them requirements in the promotion process.

From our experience, managers who lack "people" skills have more difficulty with employee involvement. They simply aren't comfortable with the intense interaction that results. And again, when anything makes us uncomfortable, we tend to resist.

Managers Left Out

A final cause of management resistance is poor implementation of the employee involvement effort.

Here's a scenario for the launching of an effort. A Chief Executive Officer of one company hears about the benefits another company is reaping from their new participation program. This CEO immediately sees the possibilities for his own company and designates someone to begin implementing some form of employee involvement, such as Quality Circles. The front-liners become involved in problem-solving teams and get "turned on" to the new concepts. But somehow all of middle management has been left out of the process.

As incredible as this sounds, it is not atypical. In some programs, we've even seen the CEO on videotape telling his managers that they will "commit to and support the effort...or else," and the "or else" leaves few questions in the managers' minds about their future with the company.

Based on what you now know about resistance, it should be clear that this type of implementation is destined for problems. After all, the principles of employee involvement apply to managers as well. If the managers haven't been involved in any of the thinking that's gone into the new effort, they'll be less likely to support it. And so we again see resistance.

Whether consciously or unconsciously, some managers will obstruct the process or find fault when something doesn't work. They will then point to the CEO or to the person in charge of "that program over there" as being responsible for the problems. Since they were not part of creating the effort, they feel no responsibility for its success. The effort becomes a victim of the "not invented here" syndrome.

Another problem that arises when managers are not part of the decision-making process is that they will perceive the new effort as "the employee's program." Managers will keep their distance, feeling it has nothing to do with them.

Leaving managers out of the initial planning of the program is a serious problem, and one that needs considerable attention.

Overcoming Resistance

There are, however, ways to overcome the resistance that threatens the survival of employee involvement efforts. The next section will discuss how to overcome resistance in the workforce, in unions, and in management.

Overcoming Resistance in the Workforce

The key to overcoming resistance among the workers is to involve them in the effort as early as possible. Once their mental energies are directed away from negative thinking and toward productive solutions to problems, attitudes begin to change.

Depending on how management behaves, particularly in terms of how much visible support management provides, employees will either commit to the effort or continue to distrust it.

In my experience, front-liner resistance is really "skepticism." If we look back at Chapter 3, we see that workers are longing to "use their minds and abilities." They simply won't resist a concept that provides that opportunity, but they are intensely skeptical of management's motives and willingness to commit to such an effort.

Overcoming Resistance in Unions

If the organization's workforce, or part of it, is represented by a union, there may be some natural resistance from the union itself. What can be done to overcome this resistance?

Involve the Leadership at the Outset

Perhaps the most common failure resulting in union resistance to employee participation is not involving the union's leadership in the planning stages.

Old wounds heal slowly, and sometimes it's difficult to begin working on the same side of the table. But any organization that isn't building good relationships with its union today is oblivious to the winds of change. We simply can't afford not to work together anymore.

A union leader who represents hundreds, maybe thousands, of an organization's workers has power. And any management team that fails to recognize and respect that power is courting disaster anytime it launches a new program that involves people.

Therefore, at the outset of any worker participation program, the union's leadership should be part of the planning and administration...and not just as figureheads. Union leaders have a different perspective that can help management avoid pitfalls.

Involving the union at the outset is such an important point that the Economic Policy Council, mentioned earlier, includes it as a major recommendation for any organization implementing worker participation programs.

The Council, made up of union and business leaders from around the country, recommends: "Where unions represent the workers, the union must be involved as an equal partner from planning through implementation and evaluation of the program."[14]

Admit Management Is Most of the Problem

It's hard to argue with someone who admits a mistake. In fact, if you admit you've caused a problem and ask for help in solving it, it's hard for someone to refuse you. This has been my experience in working with union leaders.

In the construction industry, for example, it's no secret that productivity has been on a steady decline for 25 years. For most of that time, management and labor have been pointing fingers at each other, calling the other the culprit. And it is true that both share the blame...but not equally.

Quality guru Dr. Edwards Deming has shown us clearly that most quality and productivity problems are caused by the process of production, not by the workers. He also says that management is responsible for at least 80% of the performance problems in an organization.

So my policy over the years has been to own up to this fact. We tell the union leadership that management has been the major problem, but our emphasis now is on improving...and we need their help.

My experiences have reinforced my belief that people are good, and if you look for that good, you'll find it. I've never had a union leader, who was approached in this manner, refuse to support a request. In fact, there have been times when I was heading for a downfall, only to be saved by a union leader's advice.

The key, however, is honesty and sincerity. People can usually see through any attempt to manipulate them with words. But if you really believe management is the primary problem in organization performance today, and ask for the union's help, you'll get it.

Guests, Visits, and References

People tend to resist what they don't understand. Having union leaders better understand the program will help to raise their comfort levels.

Our country has gained significant experience with employee involvement, quality of work-life, and labor-management cooperation. There are numerous companies where management and unions are working hand-in-hand to make their organizations better.

One strategy for raising comfort levels is to visit such organizations, encouraging the union officials there to discuss their employee involvement experiences. An alternative strategy is to invite these union officials to your organization.

Once I provided the skeptical head of the International Brotherhood of Electrical Workers (IBEW) System Council with a list of other IBEW officials I had worked with, and encouraged him to talk with them about my work. He soon became a supporter.

The U.S. Department of Labor has expanded the function of the Bureau of Labor-Management Relations to include **Cooperative Programs**. The Bureau is a good source of information about supportive unions and union leaders.

Rank and File Members

No discussion of union resistance would be complete without addressing rank and file members. Far and away, most union members support the concepts of greater involvement in improving the organization. They are in a position to make significant contributions and to correct problems they see at their level. But occasionally there are members who resist any attempt to work closely with management.

As stated earlier, old values die hard. When you've spent a lifetime on opposite sides of the fence with management, it's difficult to see yourselves working together. Some union members have had several generations of their families working the same jobs in the same unions, and the belief system is deeply embedded.

Sometimes resisting members will form coalitions and harass other members who begin working on improvement teams. Feeling threatened by their own peers, the team members will either hold back or withdraw entirely from the effort.

This, unfortunately, begins to drive a wedge within the union, because most people want to contribute. Most people are frustrated by poor work procedures and practices and want desperately to change them. Now management is no longer the barrier to this change, their fellow members are. And the frustration continues.

Union leaders should act swiftly and decisively to squelch this resistance. It's destructive not only to the company, but to the union. In so doing, union leadership will have the support of the overwhelming majority of their membership.

113

Overcoming Resistance in Management

With rare exceptions, it's difficult to pinpoint the exact cause of a particular manager's resistance to employee involvement. In fact, there's probably more than one cause of the resistance.

The following ideas for overcoming resistance are, therefore, intended to address all causes of resistance at once.

Implementation Plan

As stated earlier, a poor implementation plan will cause resistance, so considerable attention should be paid to it. Although Chapter 6 is devoted to the subject of implementation, in this section I'd like to discuss those aspects of implementation that relate to overcoming resistance in management.

The implementation plan should allow sufficient time for managers and supervisors to understand and gain confidence in the concepts of employee involvement. Even though it may be tempting to create employee performance improvement teams immediately, this temptation should be resisted in favor of obtaining long-term growth through a committed management team. Middle managers and front-line supervisors will be depended on for the ultimate success of the effort. The failure rate mentioned earlier attests to the necessity of obtaining the unqualified support of all management personnel.

Therefore, depending on the size and character of the organization, from **one to two years** should be allotted to properly prepare the management team.

Keeping in mind the need for management to support the concepts of employee involvement, those responsible for initiating the program should:

- Design strategies for management involvement
- Create dissatisfaction with the status quo
- Raise comfort levels
- Be consistent
- Be intolerant of insubordination

Design Strategies for Management Involvement

Tell me, I'll forget.
Show me, I may remember.
But involve me, and I'll understand.

In these few words lie the essence and value of involvement. Managers are people, too, and have a need to be involved. Therefore, any implementation plan should allow time and create mechanisms for managers to have input into the effort's design and implementation.

As managers gain understanding and confidence in the concepts, they'll be in a more knowledgeable position to train their own subordinates.

Mechanisms for involving managers and supervisors include:

- Initiating dialogue meetings between senior and subordinate managers
- Holding planning sessions, assigning various aspects of the effort to teams of managers
- Organizing working retreats
- Setting up management problem-solving teams or quality circles

- Enlisting managers as trainers
- Encouraging management field trips to other organizations
- Enrolling managers in societies such as the Association for Quality and Participation

Create Dissatisfaction with the Status Quo

D. L. "Dutch" Landen of D.L. Landen & Associates says that before any meaningful change can occur, three elements must exist:[15]

1. Being dissatisfied with the status quo
2. Knowing what you want to change to
3. Knowing the steps in the change process

When I first heard this, I didn't think much about it. Then I began to consider the difficulties some employee involvement efforts were having in light of these elements.

We certainly knew what we were changing to (a more participatory environment), and we had laid out the steps in the process. Maybe what was missing was dissatisfaction with the status quo.

I honestly don't believe we've paid enough attention to changing people's attitudes about the **need** to improve the way we work. What would the catalyst be? What would make people want to change from something comfortable to something different, unknown, and possibly threatening?

In some industries, such as auto and steel, the catalyst is simple...survival. But in other industries, there just isn't the urgency. And why should a manager whose organization is profitable and healthy feel a need to change? What should those initiating an employee involvement effort do to create this need to change?

The simple answer is "they should get smart." They should begin acquiring information about the state of our economy. They should read government studies showing the sad state of America's position in world competition and the hardcore numbers on productivity. They should read books, such as John Naisbett's *Megatrends*, that show the major changes taking place in our society. They should read reports that clearly demonstrate our inability to predict and control costs of federal programs like Medicare and Social Security. They should listen to the discussions of what will happen to the "baby boomer" generation when they are ready to retire. They should re-read Chapter 2. They should read the studies that show the problems associated with a burgeoning national debt. They should study the reports showing clearly that in good times or bad, customers will buy, and pay a premium for, those products they perceive to have a relatively higher quality. They should buy the videotape, *Quality Circles: For My Own Cause* and see firsthand the intensity with which Japanese workers pursue quality. They should get a group of people together and recount their own "customer horror stories."

No matter how good the organization is, it can always be better. They should take this mass of information and ask the people in their organization what they intend to do about it...ask them what kind of world they want to leave for their children. Will their sons or daughters be able to buy a house in the year 2000? It's a sure bet they'll stir some emotions, discomfort, and dissatisfaction with the status quo. And that's what they want.

I'm constantly amazed that, in our country, we have to struggle to make these improvement programs work. I think it's because we get caught up in so much pettiness, me-ism, and bureaucracy instead of getting on with the business of making something better.

From experience, I know that those initiating the change to an employee involvement effort will be able to create discomfort and dissatisfaction with the status quo. Most people already know a lot of the information mentioned above, but when someone brings it to the surface, there will be a relevance and a meaning for the change.

Raise Comfort Levels

The implementation strategy should include a concerted effort to raise management's comfort level with employee involvement.

When the workforce is invited to participate in general problem-solving and management decisions, problems will surface, and managers will naturally fear that senior management will blame the supervisor or manager in charge for those problems. This fear will be heightened if the organization has a history of such behavior.

To raise the comfort level, senior management must **establish a policy of attacking the problem, not the person.** It must be instilled in everyone to look upon the problem as an opportunity for improvement, not as a screwup in need of fixing.

When problems are uncovered, possibly by employee improvement teams, the supervisors may feel responsible. Their level of confidence will determine how they'll view the situation.

First, if insecure, they may blame themselves for the problem, saying it shouldn't have happened. They may feel they used poor judgment or planned poorly. If they feel very threatened, they may blame someone else.

But other supervisors, with more open, confident personalities, would look at the problem as a real opportunity to make things better. Very confident supervisors might even thank the team for bringing the problem to light, clearly demonstrating their focus is on improving.

Senior management can do a lot to instill this type of confidence in managers by letting them know that it's OK to screw up once in a while. In fact, this should be part of the orientation at initial meetings with managers and supervisors. Nobody's perfect, so say so. The focus is on improving, not blaming.

Another way of preparing managers is **exposing them to the brainstorming process.** Brainstorming is a powerful technique used by teams to generate as many thoughts as possible. It's the only time a team is looking for quantity over quality. Therefore, lots of ideas should be generated.

In a case we discussed earlier, the supervisor was horrified by the length of the list of problems in his group. But if he had been prepared, there would have been no surprises. Therefore, when managers and supervisors are oriented, brainstorming and what to expect from it should be on the agenda.

Another way to raise comfort levels is to **provide training in areas such as communication, interpersonal relations, personality types, personal values, and other such human factors.** People have a great need to understand themselves and others. When they understand the factors that drive behavior, they feel more comfortable with other people.

For example, in training programs we run, we discuss personal values—where our values or beliefs come from and how

119

they affect our behavior with others. Then we use a simple Values Clarification Exercise to show how different we all are, and how hard it is to come to agreement when our values differ. For the first time in their lives, the trainees understand the causes of many arguments and disagreements they've had and the reasons for the resulting frustration.

At lunch one day during a training session, I was sitting with some trainees discussing competition in the world. An argument was brewing over the quality of American cars versus the quality of Japanese cars. One 35-year-old engineer commented that he only bought Japanese cars today; a 40-year-old manager said he did likewise. At that point, the hand of a 59-year-old supervisor started twitching, and a few seconds later he commented, "I lived through Pearl Harbor." The atmosphere got a little tense, so I asked them to recall this conversation when we discussed values later in the day.

Later that afternoon, after we had completed the training session on values, I told the whole group about the lunchtime discussion. The three trainees who had been involved all smiled and agreed that their value systems had entered into the argument. Although they hadn't said so, the younger men had been looking at the older supervisor as an "obstinate old fool." After all, he had been arguing pretty fervently in support of American cars, and they knew clearly that American cars were inferior in quality to Japanese cars.

But after the training on values, they could understand the source of his beliefs. As a young boy, he had seen American sailors brutally massacred at Pearl Harbor. It was an image he would carry with him the rest of his life...an event that would forever affect his behavior concerning anything Japanese.

Instead of three people walking away from the interchange upset and frustrated, they could now understand each other's position. They didn't necessarily agree with each other, but at least they could understand.

The same kinds of misunderstandings and disagreements occur when implementing employee involvement concepts. The more we know about ourselves and the behavior of others, the more comfortable we become with the change.

Another excellent method of raising comfort levels is to **bring in speakers from other organizations** who are running successful participation efforts. They will generally relate their personal experiences, admitting their initial fears and concerns and discussing how, with time, those concerns never materialized.

One such person is former Campbell Soup Company Executive Vice President Lewis Springer. Springer's youthful exuberance belies his 40 years with the company. He is an avid supporter of the employee's role in the Total Quality Process, but even he will confess that he underwent a significant transformation when he changed his thinking away from traditional management methods. With respect to employee involvement, he evangelistically refers to himself as "Born-Again Springer," and is an excellent spokesperson for the concepts.

Allowing managers to **visit other organizations** that have successful employee involvement programs is another way to raise comfort levels.

One supervisor we know at Public Service Electric & Gas Company readily admits he was skeptical until he visited a sister utility using employee involvement teams. He was part of a management committee looking into the feasibility of using employee involvement concepts at PSE&G, and was one of the more vocal opponents. The committee had already heard talks from outsiders and had visited other companies, but it was only when he saw a team of electricians enthusiastically analyzing problems at Baltimore Gas & Electric that his comfort level rose. Something just clicked.

Another way to raise comfort levels is to **let managers and supervisors experience the feel of working on improvement teams.** Being on a team of managers and supervisors allows them to learn the problem-solving process, group dynamics, team leadership, and other such skills that their subordinates will be learning. They will not only be solving organizational problems, but also developing confidence in their ability to teach and lead subordinates in the concepts.

Comfort levels tend to rise in a high information environment. When initiating the program, talk openly about successes and failures, what works and what doesn't, and what people should expect as they move further into worker participation concepts.

Finally, those who are initiating the effort should **be sensitive to the needs of managers and supervisors as they undergo change in their organizations.** If there is one area we fail at most often, it is being attuned to other human beings. Do we care if they're worried? Do we care if they have frustrations and feel stressed? Do we care if their latent insecurity is rising to the surface? We should. Because these all affect behavior and performance.

One manager we worked with was having a considerable amount of discomfort with his employee involvement team, and although he went through the motions of support, his heart wasn't in it. After almost a year had gone by, the team's facilitator began approaching him to probe for the sources of his discomfort. Several one-on-one discussions revealed some concerns he had about the new team.

First, he didn't understand the list of problems generated by the team. Some of the items appeared trivial and he couldn't understand why they would put them on the list. Second, he was uncomfortable with the published minutes of the team's meetings. He clearly felt that some of the topics discussed by the team were his responsibility, not theirs. He was also concerned that his boss, an assistant vice president, would wonder about his leadership ability if he saw the list.

The facilitator, recognizing that these were normal concerns, could now begin raising the manager's comfort level.

He first explained that the items on the team's list were very normal; in fact, they were much better than those of other departments in the company. He assured the manager that he wouldn't experience any repercussions from the published minutes; in fact, they would actually enhance his image in the department as a progressive, confident manager. As for the concern about the vice president, the facilitator simply said, "What would his list look like if his staff began brainstorming problems?"

Learning that the team's actions were perfectly normal significantly allayed the manager's anxiety. Over the next few months, his relationship with the team blossomed, which in turn helped the team to develop more confidence.

The message here is sensitivity. The facilitator was sensitive to the needs of the manager and responded accordingly.

Unfortunately, in the world of business, we seem to shun this type of human contact. Emotion and business do not mix under "Scientific Management." But it's ludicrous to believe that people leave their feelings and emotions on the front step as they enter the workplace.

Being sensitive to the natural concerns of managers implementing employee involvement is essential in raising comfort levels.

Be Consistent

American management seems to tire quickly of new management techniques. So the response of middle management and the workforce is, "If we wait long enough, maybe it'll go away." The same thing happens in employee involvement.

Certain managers and supervisors sit quietly on the sidelines, uninvolved in the effort. Eventually, senior management takes on new priorities, and the effort begins to die a natural death. Those on the sidelines invested nothing, so they lose nothing.

However, in organizations with strong employee involvement efforts, senior management's behavior is consistent. Senior management is intent on making participation part of the operating behavior of the organization, so they set the standard. Month after month the sideliners see senior management in this role, and eventually they realize that if they don't get on the train, it may leave without them.

Be Intolerant of Insubordination

One issue that has puzzled me relates to what I call insubordination. Some brash supervisors and managers openly oppose the new employee involvement effort, yet experience no repercussions for their actions. The message received by the organization is, "Management mustn't be serious about employee involvement. Why else would they let them get away with it?"

My policy is normally to work these things out with the offenders. I try to convince them that it's in their best interest and in the best interest of the company. (See Dissatisfaction with the Status Quo.)

But occasionally there comes a time when enough is enough, and stronger measures are needed. Supervisors who don't respond should be separated from the organization.

In a management orientation on employee involvement, a vice president we know was asked, "What would you do if a manager or supervisor refused to use the concepts of employee involvement?"

He replied, "Times are changing and our organization must also change and improve. If an organization sets a direction for the future, it depends on all hands pulling together to support that direction. Anyone who does not support it is out of step with where it's going, and therefore, must leave."

Another senior manager we know used an appropriate metaphor to say the same thing. He told an uncooperative manager, "The wind's blowing in a set direction, and that's the direction the ship is going. If you don't want to find yourself left in the water, you'd better climb on board."

Insubordination must be dealt with firmly or it will undermine the entire effort.

125

Final Comments on Resistance in Management

What has happened in America in the last 200 years is outstanding, and our basic management principles have served to bring much of this about.

But the system today is out of step with a vastly changed marketplace and a vastly changed workforce. Adopting the concepts of quality, customer service, and innovation, all supported by a **foundation of people involvement,** is being accepted as the only viable way to compete in this marketplace.

By now it should be clear that there are some very basic reasons why managers and supervisors may resist the concepts of participative management. The better we understand the human problems associated with change, the more likely it is that we'll be able to respond to those problems.

Summary of Resistance

Resistance to change is normal. Resistance to employee involvement is to be expected, and it will be felt most in the management ranks.

In the workforce, resistance is caused by the **credibility gap** with management. Employees simply don't believe management is serious. They have seen many programs come and go, and believe this effort will be the same. This resistance is usually overcome easily, however, as the workers become involved and the effort takes hold and produces results.

With union leadership, the resistance stems from its adversarial position with management. Union leaders are usually skeptical and mistrusting of management's motives, and in some cases, rightly so. However, this resistance is usually overcome at the outset with open, honest dialogue about improving the organization and by reinforcing the union's role in the effort.

But with management, the problem of resistance is more serious, because management holds the key to implementing and sustaining any change in an organization. Managers and supervisors are in control. They are the leaders, the models of how the organization is to operate. Therefore, any resistance in management will have disastrous effects on the success of the employee involvement effort.

Resistance in management stems from a reluctance to share power, give up control, expose oneself to possible criticism, or reveal one's faults. Causes of resistance include:

- Ego
- Insecurity
- Personal Values
- Prior Training
- Management Not "High Touch"
- Managers Left Out

To overcome resistance in management, the organization should:

- Design the change process to include significant management involvement in its implementation
- Create significant dissatisfaction with the status quo, stimulating a need for change
- Provide support to raise comfort levels with the new concepts
- Be consistent in the pursuit of participative management, continuously modeling the desired behavior

- Be intolerant of insubordination, and deal immediately and decisively with flagrant resisters

Resistance to a concept that clearly produces positive results for an organization doesn't make sense anymore. There's just too much left to do.

5 Management Support Behaviors

Who teaches me for a day is my father for a lifetime.

—Chinese proverb

The process of change from traditional management concepts to employee involvement is a process of growth ...growth for the organization and growth for the individual. And as the organization evolves, it remains vital and healthy.

In our training programs, as we've done here, we discuss the power of management to influence the character of the organization. We discuss how intently front-liners observe every action of managers in their day-to-day routines, looking for signals of how to behave. And we talk about how, since managers have so much influence on behavior in the organization, their actions in supporting and leading the change to employee involvement are crucial to its success.

But we frequently get questions from managers and supervisors asking what specifically they should do. "Should I attend my team's meetings or will they feel intimidated by my presence?" "Can I suggest topics for them to work on?" "Shouldn't I just stay in the background and let their natural thought processes occur?" "What if I have a busy week and just can't allocate time to the effort?"

Many in management are sincerely puzzled, at least initially, about how to act in an employee involvement atmosphere. But there are specific behaviors that demonstrate that management not only supports the change but is leading the way toward the organization's improvement. So let's look at these behaviors. What specifically should the manager or supervisor do?

Supportive Attitude

The first thing managers should do is look within themselves and assess their own feelings about employee involvement. What they feel inside will be manifested in their behavior outside. And particularly if the managers come under any pressure, those inner feelings are very likely to surface.

Dr. Wayne Dyer uses an analogy with an orange to describe the importance of our inner feelings. He says, "If you squeeze an orange, what comes out? Orange juice. Why? Because that's what's inside."[1] So it is with people. Whatever feelings we carry around inside us will eventually come to the surface.

If managers have some doubts about employee involvement, that's OK. They should reread the "ugly facts" about our economy, reread the success stories to see what's possible when we begin involving our people in problem-solving and innovation. At least they should be willing to give employee involvement every benefit of the doubt.

Many people talk about "management commitment" and how important it is to the success of employee involvement. I agree, but it's hard to be committed to something you've never tried before. Commitment will come when the managers see results, both for the organization and for themselves personally. But the results will come only if they nurture the process. Therefore, managers and supervisors must develop a sincerely supportive attitude.

Managers as Role Models

Since people tend to emulate the behaviors of their leaders, managers should be aware that they are role models for the process.

This may be the most difficult supportive behavior to adopt. As discussed earlier, we've spent this entire century teaching managers that their job was to do the thinking and labor's job was to carry out orders. Now we're changing the rules. Now we're asking labor to think with us. So this "first generation" of participative managers will find it difficult, if not impossible, to change overnight. Learned behavior is difficult to unlearn.

Nevertheless, they must. Employee involvement means involving people in the thinking process...not just an hour a week, but all week. A manager or supervisor makes many decisions that are appropriate for employee input. Consulting an employee about a change in work assignment, seeking advice from a front-liner who has special knowledge of some aspect of the work, getting input from the group during a staff meeting...all are forms of employee involvement.

Unfortunately, some managers forget this. One manager we know preaches employee involvement, then sporadically changes work assignments, job descriptions, and work group priorities without ever consulting the people affected. As a result, they have a scornful attitude. As far as they're concerned, he doesn't have even the slightest consideration for their involvement.

It's easy for managers to make this mistake. That's why it's important that they be sensitive to any situation that may lend itself to the involvement of their subordinates. Eventually managers will see the quality of their decisions improving and commitment building in their organization as a result of the participation of their subordinates.

Managers as Trainers

This is a recommendation that may get me into trouble with some managers. I can just hear them saying, "Me do the training? When have I got the time?"

But I don't think managers have any greater purpose than to train their subordinates in high performance thinking.

Apparently, Carolina Power & Light agrees. When implementing their quality improvement/employee involvement effort, they had supervisors do the initial orientations with their subordinates, and managers serve as "adjunct faculty" in the training program. By design, management played a significant part in the entire training effort.

When managers do the training, they serve as powerful role models. And by doing the training, they will probably become better practitioners in the workplace. In other words, they will probably "practice what they preach."

Perhaps the most common complaint with training programs today is that the behaviors being taught are not modeled by management in the workplace. Put another way, management isn't practicing what the training programs are teaching.

One frustrated trainer put it to us this way. He said, "We take our young supervisors away for two weeks for special management training. It's very expensive. Then they go back to work and see their managers doing the opposite of what they learned. Which do you think has more impact, the two weeks they spend with us, or the other 50 weeks they spend with their managers?"

When the managers themselves do the training, however, there is never a conflict between theory and practice.

Managers as Facilitators

The term "facilitator" as used in employee involvement refers to the person who helps a team of people through some problem-solving process. The facilitator teaches problem-solving techniques as well as aspects of group dynamics. Facilitators are observers of the group process. They observe what's going well and what isn't, then help the team to make adjustments.

In most organizations, facilitators are a separate group. Maybe they're set up as the "Employee Involvement Department" or the "Quality Circle Program" with their own staffs. Regardless of what they are called, they are usually separate from other departments.

I can speak from experience about being a facilitator in a separate department. I sometimes felt awkward as the facilitator, as though I were intruding in the affairs of another department. I felt that I was doing a job that should have been done by someone internal to that department.

Some teams I worked with became loyal to my department rather than to their own. While this was understandable—here was my department coaching them through problems and helping them be a more unified team—it seemed to me that we were defeating our own purpose. I always felt sad that the same feeling of loyalty wasn't going to their own department.

So the next recommendation is for managers to act as facilitators of their own teams. Again, I hear the cries of "No time!" But there are always compromises.

A manager could lead a short-term task force once a year. Or facilitate one quality circle for a few weeks. Or facilitate each <u>new</u> team for a couple of months. There are variations.

In the work I did facilitating teams, I would often find myself saying, "If only the manager could hear what I'm hearing." Many times I was tempted to videotape team meetings because I felt the comments were so revealing of the organization's problems. **These are the comments managers need to hear.**

I know that some will say that if a manager is present, the comments won't come out. Maybe at first. But when team members become accustomed to the manager's presence, they feel more comfortable discussing deep-felt issues. It just takes a little time.

I recently witnessed this change in an engineering organization. Several months ago, the appearance of the vice president during the meeting would cause a mysterious hush to fall over the members. But his attendance at a meeting recently did nothing to inhibit the candid conversation.

MBWA

How managers spend their time says a lot about their priorities. Do they spend their time reviewing memos, letters, budget revisions, or computer reports in their offices, or guiding, coaching, helping, and talking to their subordinates?

MBWA, or Management by Wandering Around, has received a lot of attention in recent years. And well it should. Some aspects of the business just don't show up in a printed report.

In terms of employee involvement, MBWA becomes a major activity, not in time, but effect.

Visits to Teams

Probably the most effective use of managers' time is visiting employee involvement teams in their departments (although we wouldn't rule out visiting teams and committees in other departments as well). By visiting the team during one of its meetings, a manager is saying in effect, "What you're doing here is important to me, and I value your contribution." Again, the manager's visit may be intimidating at first, but this intimidation usually diminishes as the visits grow in frequency.

The length of the visit is unimportant. Merely stopping in for five or ten minutes will convey the message. However, if time is available, the manager can participate in the team's work—usually the team will invite the manager to participate in the discussions. In fact, it's important for this to happen as often as possible. The manager usually possesses knowledge that will be of benefit to the team's project.

Managers should, however, be cognizant of their behavior with the teams. They've delegated responsibility to the teams and shouldn't take over when they're there. The managers are there to help, nurture, and advise without directing. Unless they suffer from severe ego problems (see Chapter 4), managers should appreciate the independent actions their teams are taking to improve the department. They don't, therefore, want to take away the team's authority when they visit.

One of the most effective uses of MBWA I've ever observed was when I attended a team training session at Weirton Steel Company in Weirton, West Virginia. At the end of the three days of training, in walked President/CEO Robert Loughead, two executive vice presidents, and the president of the Independent Steel Workers Union. For the next hour, team members discussed with them their reactions to the training, their feelings about management and union commitment to the program, and their ideas on how they could improve the company. I later learned that these top leaders do this with <u>every</u> training session. In an 8000-person organization this is not insignificant.

The effect on the team members was dramatic. They were given an opportunity to discuss important issues with the top people in the company. It also became crystal clear just how important their employee involvement effort was. (Not incidentally, Weirton Steel's profits have grown steadily over the last several years while many other plants have closed.)

The importance of senior manager visits to teams should not be underestimated.

I once worked with a team that had been in existence for about a year. For some reason, the supervisors in the department would not attend any of the team's meetings. This was interpreted by the members as a lack of interest, and they became resentful. They couldn't understand why their "leaders" wouldn't support something that was bene-fiting the company.

One day during a particularly productive meeting, I ducked out and asked the vice president if he could spare ten minutes to visit the team. He came to the meeting and con-tributed some new ideas. He actually spent no more than ten minutes with them. Later they included his name on their minutes as a guest at the meeting.

Within three weeks, their supervisors, who had never before attended a meeting, began coming on a regular basis. The relationship between team members and supervisors improved, and the team became even more productive. All from a ten-minute visit by the vice president.

These visits are vitally important. When starting their quality circle program several years ago, the West Jersey Health System of Camden, New Jersey, monitored the frequency of management visits to circle meetings. Three of the four hospi-tals were doing well in their implementation, but the fourth was experiencing problems with the circles. The circles were progressing slowly, and member absenteeism was high.

An analysis of the figures showed that the fourth hospi-tal had the lowest rate of management involvement. In fact, management visits to circle meetings was very low compared to the other hospitals.

When this fact was presented to the hospital's manage-ment, they began to increase their involvement. Ultimately, the performance of their circles improved and fell in line with the others.

Visits to team meetings may be the single most impor-tant way for managers to show how important the work of the teams are.

137

Visits to Team Leaders and Members

Another way of showing support is by making special visits to team leaders and members. Some perceive the time spent by employee involvement teams as "break time," but it is work. Members, and especially team leaders, put considerable effort into making their teams productive.

When the manager visits a team leader or member on a frequent basis, the visit provides recognition for the work they are doing.

High Information Environment

MBWA managers create a high information environment. They are always "stirring the pot." They talk with subordinates frequently about what's going on in their teams. They encourage discussions about the failures as well as the successes, which helps people feel more comfortable about venturing into the unknown.

These managers encourage ideas. If the company has a suggestion program, they constantly promote the idea of improvement through innovation, and encourage and assist people to submit ideas.

People are more comfortable and productive in this "high information" environment.

"15 Critical Minutes"

It would be unrealistic to believe that managers could give a lot of time every week to MBWA devoted to employee involvement.

However, there is a minimum amount of time that the manager must allocate each week in direct support of the employee involvement effort, and that amount I call the "15 Critical Minutes." The 15 Critical Minutes is a quick visit to a task team this week. It's three five-minute discussions with team members next week. It's a visit to a quality circle the next week. It's a concept that says no week will go by without direct support of some kind.

I've watched teams wilt and die from neglect because their managers "could not find the time" to make a visit. As unfair as it seems, team members will interpret the nonverbal messages as they will. And when the manager appears to have lost interest, the interest wanes also in the team.

It astonishes me, but people need their leaders. They need to see and hear their leaders. Even in construction, where work is temporary, the workers would frequently comment that they would like to see the bosses once in a while. Who are they? What do they look like?

That's why I feel so strongly about the 15 Critical Minutes. It's not the amount of time you spend, but how you spend it that's important. Unrelenting consistency, week in and week out.

Quick Action on Recommendations

Occasionally a subordinate or a team will have an idea that needs action from the manager. This presents an excellent opportunity for managers to demonstrate strong support.

If the manager moves quickly to put the idea into action, the team again gets a message that they are important. The team knows the manager will act decisively when presented with good ideas, and so are encouraged to challenge themselves further. Most facilitators see a direct correlation between management responsiveness and team productivity.

Recognition

Managers must find ways of recognizing the accomplishments of their subordinates. Recognition was discussed in depth in Chapter 3 as a major motivator. All human beings need recognition.

Recognition of employee involvement accomplishments can take many forms. A simple visit to a team meeting to say "Thank you" may be all that's needed. If the team has worked particularly hard on something, the manager may take them out to lunch. The manager could set up a competition for productivity, and reward the winning team by taking them to a national conference of the Association for Quality and Participation.

Publicity in the company newsletter, an article in the community newspaper or trade magazines, lunches with company executives, days off with pay, small gifts of appreciation, certificates of appreciation, appreciation days, the list is endless. Recognition can take many forms, and sends a strong message of support.

Union Leaders

Although we have concentrated mainly on management support, union leaders should also adopt supportive behaviors.

Workers represented by a union will sometimes feel a conflict between their new involvement in improving the organization and the old standards of the past. They will, therefore, be looking toward their union leaders for direction. These leaders should send clear-cut messages of support and cooperation with a new improvement effort.

Union leaders should be invited by management to visit team meetings, individual members, and team leaders. They should keep abreast of team developments and provide constant reassurances to union members that their work to support the company is vital.

Union meetings should also reinforce the company's direction and show unified support for improvement.

The standards of the past are no longer valid in a world economy. We can only survive by working together. This message must be clear to all union members.

Final Words on Support Behaviors

Employee involvement cannot survive, or at best, will only limp along without the active, visible involvement of the organization's management. Management's role in creating a vital and productive improvement effort is critical.

Some of the ideas we've discussed in this chapter may be unfamiliar to some managers. MBWA, for example, is a new technology that some people find uncomfortable at first.

However, the more frequently managers perform MBWA, the more likely that both managers and subordinates will become comfortable in their new roles.

As I said in the previous chapter, it's absolutely essential that management spend time preparing themselves for the introduction of employee involvement. They must take time to become knowledgeable in the people skills as well as in the task skills of problem-solving and innovating. If this preparation time is invested, managers and supervisors will be more inclined to practice the supportive behaviors discussed here.

6 Setting Up the Process

The foundations for a better tomorrow
must be laid today.

The primary emphasis in this book has been on the influence of management on the employee involvement process. The way management behaves in a participative environment will ultimately determine the program's success or failure. Assuming the preceding chapters have adequately made this point, the obvious question becomes, "OK, I understand my importance in the process. Now how do we get started?" Or if an organization already has an employee involvement effort the question might be, "What adjustments should we make to improve it?"

The purpose of this chapter is to discuss the principles of running an employee involvement process. Notice that I say "principles" rather than "the nuts and bolts" of administering such an effort. That's because every organization is different from the next, and each must determine the best structure for its operation. There are some very basic principles, however, that should guide the development of that structure.

Getting Started

When an organization decides to create (or re-create) an employee involvement environment, it must begin at the beginning with the basic questions of who, what, why, when, and how. So let's look at these questions.

"Who" Is Involved?

The first thing senior management will want to discuss is simply how to begin. A multitude of questions will result. So who should be involved in these initial discussions?

First of all, **every senior manager** should be involved. They are the leaders, they are the creators of change and, therefore, should be involved in policy decisions regarding the new process.

These managers will most likely be older and have seniority in the organization; they may, therefore, misunderstand and resent (and resist) the need for employee involvement in decision-making. As we've explained earlier, involving these individuals early in the process will lessen that resistance.

If the organization's workforce is represented by a union, the **union leader(s)** should be involved at the outset. As discussed in Chapter 4, there is a natural mistrust between managements and their unions that may result in outright resistance by the union if the leaders are not involved early. Additionally, the union leadership will bring a different, but needed, perspective to the planning table that will enhance the final product.

Finally, a cross-section of the remaining **managers, supervisors, and front-liners** should have input into the planning effort. As mentioned earlier, the organization will go through a "credibility phase." If the workforce understands that the new process is not simply another management-imposed program, but rather a collaborative effort to improve the organization, it will be better received.

Representatives can be picked at random from the workforce and serve on management planning committees. Other methods to involve more of the workforce include:

- Holding open forums to discuss the planning effort
- Conducting surveys using key questions raised during planning
- Setting up specific subcommittees to address various aspects of process implementation and operation
- Having managers and supervisors discuss the effort at staff meetings

The purpose of participative management is involvement. A good way to set the tone for involvement is by using it at the outset. Involve as many people as possible in the initial planning stages.

Mary Kay Ash, creator of the enormously successful Mary Kay Cosmetics, states simply: "People will support that which they help to create."

Enough said.

"What" Are We Doing?

The "what" can be expressed as questions about what the organization is creating.

What is employee involvement?

What is the organization's goal, purpose, desired outcome?

It's important that everyone understand that the organization is not just simply creating "an employee involvement program." What is being created is:

- A workplace culture that emphasizes the importance of people in continuously improving the organization
- A climate that fosters risk-taking by looking into the "nooks and crannies" for potential improvements or breakthroughs
- A process of managing people that releases their ultimate potential for the good of the organization and the fulfillment of the individual
- A process of directing creative energy toward a purposeful objective

Looked at in this manner, employee involvement becomes an even more important process in managing the organization.

"Why" Do It?

The senior planning team (comprised of senior managers, union leaders, and some front-liners) should begin discussing why they are undertaking this new management approach. What are the reasons for the change?

More than likely, they will discuss:
- The organization's future
- Their competition in the marketplace
- The need for more quality, productivity, innovation, or customer satisfaction
- Improvement of the workplace climate
- Personal growth and development
- Employee morale/motivation
- Higher profits
- Job security
- Greater contribution to state and country
- Business responsibility to future generations

Each organization will have its own agenda, as it should. In the case of a battered steel company, the agenda may be simply survival. The planning team should define as precisely as it can those reasons for implementing the employee involvement process. People will have a need to know, and spelling out the reasons will help in the development of a vision and a philosophy.

An important consideration here is what **values** are associated with the purpose. People tend to support a reason for change that conforms to moral and ethical considerations or social responsibility. Therefore, a reason based on profit or productivity may get a cool reception if other reasons of a higher order are not included.

"When" To Do It

Once an organization makes up its mind to change to an employee involvement environment, the planning mechanism goes into operation. Setting up the planning team becomes the first order of business.

The planning team should receive training in all facets of employee involvement. After the team has acquired a basic understanding of the process, they should set up a schedule for implementing the change throughout the entire organization.

Schedules vary widely among organizations, but typically include such activities as:

- Taking baseline measurements, perhaps through organization surveys
- Setting up measurement barometers to track progress
- Conducting management training in the philosophy and concepts
- Involving management in problem-solving teams or quality circles to provide experience in the process
- Running pilot teams with front-liners
- Holding orientations for the entire workforce
- Training new teams or team leaders in the problem-solving process and group dynamics
- Assessing progress periodically

Organizations vary widely in their strategies for implementation. Weirton Steel Corporation, for example, trains all members of their Employee Participation Groups (EPG) in an intensive three-day session. After the training, a group then begins working on problems in its area. Training all members in this fashion gives <u>all</u> group members professional training before they begin work. It also serves as a teambuilding experience for the group. However, with 8000 employees, the process is slow, and it has taken Weirton Steel several years to implement it. Their philosophy has been to go slow and steady and develop effective teams.

Other organizations will train only the team leaders, then have them train their respective groups. The quality of member training is compromised to a degree, but the process of implementing teams is faster.

Then there are a few organizations that have waved a magic wand and proclaimed that, as of the next day, every employee will be in a problem-solving team. Implementation is instantaneous, but the resulting culture shock is severe. We don't recommend this type of implementation.

As the failure rate has grown, we've learned how important it is to allow sufficient time for management personnel to learn and become proficient in the process. This means that managers should receive training in problem-solving and group dynamics and have opportunities to practice their new skills in teams before the workforce begins participating en masse. (Reread Chapter 4 on "Resistance.") The point is that the planning team should schedule sufficient time for management's thorough indoctrination.

A change to employee involvement is a radical change in the operating behavior of the organization. The planning team should be patient when developing an implementation schedule. It took many years to develop the current workplace culture, and it shouldn't be expected to change overnight. It would, therefore, be reasonable to allow one to two years for a management "break-in" period before creating teams throughout the organization.

"How" To Change

The biggest question in the "who, what, why, when, and how" is how to change. How can the organization make the transition successful?

First of all, the planning team, by its very make-up, will have a lot of talent. In my experience, they usually cover many of the important subjects that need to be included. What I would like to focus on in this section are some of the important considerations that tend to be overlooked.

Management Training

Often management feels they are above the need for training in the concepts. For example, they have been problem-solving and leading meetings for years, so why should they receive training in these topics?

The answer is because 1. They are serving as the role models for the process, and 2. They need to be knowledgeable in the techniques and language the workforce will be learning. For example, if an employee team begins talking about politicking, brute force solutions, multivoting, or force field analysis, it helps if the manager knows what they're talking about.

So in what subjects might management receive training? Subjects discussed in this book will serve as a start:

- What employee involvement is
- Evolution of management thinking
- The ugly facts about America
- The employee's role in quality, customers, and innovation
- How the workforce is changing

- Needs and motivation
- Job enrichment
- Self-fulfilling prophecy
- The subconscious mind
- Effects of frustration
- Resistance to employee involvement
- Management support techniques

In addition to these, management should receive instruction in the theory and practice of the skills they'll be teaching to the workforce.

- A sound problem-solving process and techniques
- Group theory
- Group dynamics
- Human behavior
- Communication
- Meeting effectiveness
- Team measurement and evaluation
- Presentation skills

The response to this will likely be that they don't have time for the training, and certainly don't have time to form management teams to practice the skills. But again, it's like the man who sells the Fram oil filters who says, "You can pay me now, or you can pay me later." Management training is a must.

A Vision and Philosophy

The planning team, being a cross-section of the organization, is an appropriate body to develop a vision and philosophy for the organization.

The vision is a picture of what you want the organization to look like, what you want it to be. The philosophy represents the general guidelines of how you will operate. Other words that have similar meanings include goals, objectives, creed, purpose, and beliefs.

A vision gives the organization a direction, and a philosophy the operating guidelines. To reach a desired end state, all employees must know where the organization is going and by what principles or guidelines it will get there. Some examples follow:

Fiero Assembly Plant

Provide an environment for employee involvement, an atmosphere of trust, of mutual respect and human dignity so that we may achieve our common goals of high quality, mutual success, job security, and effective community relationships.

Sperry Defense Systems Division

Our Vision – *DSD is people working as a team challenged to do their best in an open atmosphere of trust, respect and concern for the individual.*

Our Beliefs – *At DSD we believe that personal growth and success of the organization are the result of:*
  – *TRUST and RESPECT for each other*
  – *Practicing SELF-DISCIPLINE*
  – *INNOVATION and RISK-TAKING*
  – *ANTICIPATING and MANAGING CHANGE*
  – *CUSTOMER SATISFACTION*
These are the responsibility of every employee.

Monsanto Silicon Modernization Project

To create an atmosphere of open communication and active participation so that we can better utilize the talents, skills, and inherent creativity of our people.

152

The visions in these statements are clear:
   "environment for employee involvement"
   "trust, mutual respect, human dignity"
   "high quality, mutual success, job security"
   "community relationships"
   "people working as a team"
   "atmosphere of trust, respect, and concern"
   "an atmosphere of open communication and active participation"

These statements conjure up a feeling of working together in a harmonious environment.

The operating principles include:
   "trust and respect for each other"
   "practicing self discipline"
   "innovation and risk taking"
   "anticipating and managing change"
   "customer satisfaction"

These principles give an organization a standard of behavior, and act as a strong motivator for the desired behavior. This, of course, assumes that these principles are being practiced at the highest levels.

The importance of vision and philosophy statements should not be underestimated. If people understand clearly the expectations of the organization and see them reinforced by senior management, then these expectations will be a driving force toward the desired result. The Theory of Self-Fulfilling Prophecy discussed earlier will apply and the organization will move steadily toward the desired end state.

An example of this is the phenomenally successful Stew Leonard's Dairy in Norwalk, Connecticut. The $100 million per year grocery store does about ten times the business of the average grocery store. The "secret" is an unwavering policy of satisfying the customer. Stew Leonard's Dairy has a very simple policy (or vision and philosophy) that states:

1. The customer is always right and
2. If the customer is ever wrong, re-read rule #1.

This may sound trite and ordinary, but if you work at Stew Leonard's you know different. Every detail of grocery shopping is slavishly attended to, and customer feedback is the cornerstone of their success. Customer suggestions are constantly monitored using suggestion boxes and customer focus groups.

But the value of the policy resides in the behavior of all employees. Stew Leonard tells the story of one young clerk who had been with the company only two weeks. A woman approached the young clerk upset about having lost a valuable pen somewhere in the store. Understanding the store's devotion to its customers, the young clerk "instinctively" pulled out three $20 gift certificates and gave them to the woman. Even though the woman had lost her pen, which was certainly not the fault of the store, the young clerk understood that here was an opportunity to create a life-long customer. Since they figure the average customer spends about $5000 a year with them, the $60 would certainly be recouped. Even more important, the woman would probably tell at least ten other people about the incident and they would become new customers.

The most important aspect of this story is that the young clerk had a clear understanding of the company's policy.

Ask yourself if a new employee in your company would act as "instinctively" in a similar situation. If not, then maybe your company's operating behavior isn't clear.

The vision and philosophy are important to achieving success and are strongly reinforced in an employee involvement atmosphere.

Measurement and Evaluation

Probably one of the most overlooked and ignored aspects of the employee involvement process is measurement and evaluation.

Most of the time, when implementing a new process, management weighs the costs versus the benefits. It's simply a customary part of conducting business. But for some reason, organizations seem reluctant to measure the effects of the employee involvement process. In a 1986 survey conducted by the Quality Circle Institute, **3 out of 4 organizations using employee involvement said they didn't collect savings-to-cost data.**[1] In our own 1988 survey of Delaware Valley businesses using employee involvement, 66% said they do not collect savings to cost data. We strongly suspect that this may be one of the causes of failure, for organizations—and particularly senior managers—cannot see the tangible benefits of the program.

A good friend of mine had created an excellent employee involvement program at a very large nuclear power construction project. The program was having a significant impact on improving work performance.

In a presentation at a conference on construction productivity, he commented that the benefits of involving employees in performance improvement were obvious; they, therefore, saw no need to measure the results. They kept no records on costs versus benefits. The sad part is that they could have documented savings in a number of areas.

155

A year later, a new management team was sent to the project, and the new construction manager wanted to see the results of their program. All they could give were stories of the improvements, not facts and statistics. There were no numbers showing that the dollars being returned to the organization far outweighed the expenses of running the program.

Not unexpectedly, the new manager began winding down the employee involvement effort, and within a couple of years it had disappeared. My friend later admitted it was a big mistake not to measure the results. In every way, he had been running one of the best employee involvement efforts in the country. But neglecting to measure the results was a fatal error.

What kinds of information can be monitored? In our experience, just about anything:

- Program costs vs. savings
- Team costs vs. savings
- Workhours saved
- Industrial safety
- Absenteeism
- Employee turnover
- Number of medical claims filed
- Number of ideas generated
- Reduction of steps in procedures
- Turnaround time
- Customer satisfaction
- Product quality
- Reduction of waste
- Number of grievances
- Order processing time
- Employee attitude

The list is almost endless. Most organizations routinely monitor some of these barometers of productivity. They will be surprised by the amount of improvement resulting from the "ripple effect" of implementing employee involvement concepts.

When we started the Monsanto project in 1980, our intent was to improve productivity. We honestly had no idea we would see turnover fall to only 1%, absenteeism to only 2%, or industrial accidents to one sixth of the national average. These were the unexpected and welcome side-effects.

When you look at published numbers on the costs versus benefits of employee involvement efforts, the numbers usually hover around a 6 to 1 return on investment. In an attempt to establish credibility, those organizations that do monitor costs are usually conservative in their estimates. Their numbers only reflect the **quantifiable results** of identified improvements and usually don't include savings from the "ripple effect." Therefore, we believe the cost benefits of employee involvement are being significantly underestimated.

For example, most organizations will informally say that their employee involvement effort was responsible for a vast improvement in employee attitude. This attitude improvement, in turn, resulted in less absenteeism, less turnover, fewer accidents, etc. But they will not attach any dollar savings to these indicators.

Admittedly, some costs are harder to quantify. How do you put a dollar figure on an employee whose better attitude toward the organization results in a 10%, 20%, or 50% improvement in work output?

Some organizations feel that measuring results may jeopardize the atmosphere they're trying to create. That is, they feel that monitoring monetary results may send a message to the workforce that management's only goal is profit. But as long as there is sufficient emphasis on improving the work environment as well as the work performance, people will respond favorably.

I think management tends to underestimate the business sense of average workers, who understand that the business must be financially successful if it is to survive. Therefore, improving the organization financially is a desirable end result. And measuring those indicators that confirm financial improvement is consistent with good management.

An overlooked aspect of measurement is the motivating effect it has on workers. When people make a contribution, whether as individuals or teams, they get satisfaction from seeing how it affects the bottom line. This is a little understood aspect of employee motivation.

For example, a team we worked with recommended that their work area be rearranged to make it more pleasant and productive. They thought of the project as an improvement to their work environment and not as something that would generate tangible savings to the company. Their facilitator, however, asked them to at least try to put a value on any improvements that might result.

The team calculated all costs to rearrange their area, and then began to look at potential savings. They were able to see that the new arrangement reduced nonproductive time within the department and reduced delays in using needed equipment. By the time they finished their evaluation, they could easily substantiate a 3 to 1 return on investment. The motivating effect this had on team members was surprising, and reaffirmed to them that cost evaluations should be a standard part of their work.

Measurement gives us a baseline from which we can begin making improvements. In the film Work Worth Doing distributed by the U. S. Department of Labor, a truck mechanic for Preston Trucking talks about life before their employee involvement process was started ten years earlier. Those were the days before they started monitoring the work, and nobody knew how long it took to do their repairs. Then they started measuring their work and found out, for example, that "it took 23.5 hours to do a B-service." Once they knew that, they could go to work on improving it. "Today," he says proudly, "it takes 11 hours to do the same service."[2]

Another form of measurement might relate to the performance of the employee involvement effort itself.

Suggestion Programs in this country are notoriously ineffective. The National Association of Suggestion Systems has performed valuable studies showing, for instance, that participation in such programs declines rapidly if the person making the suggestion doesn't receive a reply within 90 days of submittal. Knowing this, a program coordinator should monitor turnaround time with the goal of speeding it up as much as possible. Some companies we know routinely take one to three years to respond to employee suggestions, and then wonder why their workers don't participate. Measurement would help them improve these programs.

It's a common error of many efforts that their results are not quantified. The measurement of employee involvement efforts is critical to their survival.

Additional Resources

When starting employee involvement efforts, it makes sense to use all the resources available. And since employee involvement programs have been going on in this country for about twenty years, there's a wealth of information available at little or no cost.

- As mentioned earlier, the National Association of Suggestion Systems in Chicago conducts studies and publishes guidelines and recommendations that should be "required reading" by anyone operating such a program.

- The Association for Quality and Participation is another valuable resource for those interested in starting employee involvement efforts. The Association hosts two national conferences each year and makes available to its members a considerable catalog of support materials. In addition, they have many local chapters that offer excellent programs and networking opportunities.

- For organizations that feel the need for more help, there are a host of consultants coast-to-coast with many years of experience in starting or reviving employee involvement efforts. Names of these consultants can be obtained from the associations above.

- There are also many businesses willing to share their knowledge of and experience with employee involvement. With the help of some state governments, businesses are forming coalitions to set up training in employee involvement.

  One such program is the Ben Franklin Partnership Program in Pennsylvania. Some of its funds have been directed to the Philadelphia area's Quality Improvement Project and the Philadelphia Area

Council on Excellence (PACE), where member companies are receiving training in employee involvement as well as quality-related subjects.

- The federal government provides resources as well, and usually for free. The Department of Labor's Bureau of Labor-Management Relations and Cooperative Programs sponsors conferences and committees, and publishes excellent materials on all aspects of employee involvement.

There's a wealth of information available today on this subject, much of it free for the asking. Any organization wanting to start an employee involvement program or revive a previous effort should make use of these resources.

Periodic Assessments

It's essential for the planning team to build into its schedule regular assessments of progress. Too many times an organization implements an employee involvement process without following up periodically to see how it's doing.

At first these assessments should be monthly or quarterly, and later semi-annually. But the timing of the assessments is not so important; what is important is that they are done.

During these assessments the team might look at:
- Any deviation (improvement) from baseline measurements
- Management attitude toward the process
- The growth of the process; e.g., how many people have been trained and are involved
- Feedback on training regarding its effectiveness/appropriateness
- General feedback on resistance

161

- Actual vs. planned schedule of implementation
- Tangible returns (Although these may be limited the first year because people are still learning and there is a tendency to address environmental issues before productivity issues.)

Periodic assessments are essential to the growth and vitality of the new process, and must be planned from the beginning.

Renewal

After the novelty of the new program wears off, people begin to see employee involvement as part of the job. It becomes a normal part of the operating behavior of the organization, and as such, may become ordinary and less exciting.

After a few years, for example, teams might begin to feel that they have run out of topics to work on, as unbelievable as that may sound. The manager's role at this point is vital. Managers are always aware of situations in need of improvement and can help their teams with new ideas for projects.

Change is a never-ending process, and employee involvement plays a significant role in identifying needed changes. The manager needs to stimulate creativity and renew enthusiasm.

Ideas for renewal include:
- Rotating personnel on teams
- Celebrating accomplishments and breakthroughs
- Organizing team competitions
- Introducing new problem solving techniques
- Adding training in more complex "people" skills
- Loaning out employees as facilitators to the community (school boards, social organizations, religious groups, etc.)

- Running short-term, marathon-type suggestion programs with interesting incentives
- Encouraging star performers to make presentations at national conferences on employee involvement
- Frequently publicizing outstanding accomplishments

Again, the list can go on and on. The planning committee should brainstorm ideas for renewal. They usually know what's needed and when.

Returning to the question of "how" to set up the process, this section is not intended to cover the "nuts and bolts" of setting up the process. Any good management team—with the help of their union leaders and front-liners—can determine the "nuts and bolts." The topics we've just addressed are included because they tend to be overlooked. These are the topics that tend to receive little or no attention, but which are very important to a successful effort.

Final Words on Setting Up the Process

As stated earlier, employee involvement efforts have been in progress in this country for the last 20 years, and a wealth of information exists on implementation. The best approach is for the planners to educate themselves before beginning. They should visit other organizations that are using the concepts. They should attend national conferences on employee involvement. They should invite guests to speak to them on the subject. They should join the societies that focus on employee involvement. They should hire consultants if necessary.

Changing to a participative style of management involves a change in the culture of the workplace. Any

163

change of that magnitude will ultimately meet with a degree of discomfort and resistance. A well-informed planning team will be in a better position to correctly set up the process.

Epilogue

None of us is as smart as all of us.

So what is employee involvement? Is it a mechanism to involve people at all levels of an organization in the thinking process? Is it a way to generate ideas? Is it a method of solving problems? Certainly, the answer to these questions is yes.

But at this point it should be obvious that managing in a way that involves all people in the process of improving their organization goes far beyond these simple questions. Involvement sends a message of value. It sends a message of understanding that all people possess some particular talent or skill. It conveys an understanding of the uniqueness of every human being in the organization, and celebrates the creativity that resides in each of us. It is an affirmation that we are all in this together, and that no one person in the organization can ever possess more knowledge and creativity than all of us together.

Employee involvement is a concept that has the potential to dramatically change the work environment. It is a concept that clearly raises the performance of an organization. It is the single most effective weapon we have to combat the fierce competition we face in the world marketplace. It is the one resource available that may save our standard of living as we know it.

165

In this book we've discussed the precariousness of America's position in the world marketplace. We've attempted to arouse anger about America's decline, and to provoke those leading our organizations to look seriously at employee involvement as a way to reverse this decline. Our leaders hold the keys to unlock the vast potential of the workforce.

Management is feeling pressure today about our declining position in the world. Our managers are bearing the brunt of the responsibility, and some are beginning to feel guilty.

But if you look closely, it isn't really their fault. It is, rather, the result of an outdated managerial style that doesn't fit the modern workplace. It's a style that has not adapted to a greater emphasis on quality, customer service, and innovation. What's worse, it's a style that has suppressed the true potential of our productive capacity by cutting it off at the source...the worker.

Many studies have been done and a lot has been written over the last 20 years about the need to change the way we work. Unfortunately, many of the ideas seem to remain in the journals and textbooks rather than finding their way to the workplace.

As a nation of work organizations, we seem comfortable in making changes that affect work procedures, machinery, financial methods, planning concepts...in other words, those things not related to the "human" side of business.

But experience has shown us that the most significant improvements in organizations occur when the focus is on people. When the people of an organization become committed to its ideals and purpose, the effect is improvement far in excess of what may have been imagined.

166

The irony is that all we have to do is ask...ask people for their help in making our organization the best it can be.

If we do this, we just might save what our forefathers fought so hard to achieve. We might just save our way of life as we know it.

Notes

Chapter 2 So Why Change?

1. John Naisbett, *Megatrends* (New York: Warner Books, 1984) 9.

2. Naisbett, 6.

3. Naisbett, 55.

4. J. Peter Grace, "Removing the False Assumptions from Economic Policymaking," *Productivity—A National Priority* (Malibu: Pepperdine University Press, 1982) 11.

5. Grace, 9.

6. Grace, 11.

7. Naisbett, 63.

8. Naisbett, 63.

9. James R. Wilburn, "Wealth to Share," *Productivity—A National Priority* (Malibu: Pepperdine University Press, 1982) 3.

10. "High Tech Crisis Looms Over USA," *USA Today*, 8 September 1988.

11. Grace, 10.

12. Naisbett, 27.

13. *Global Competition—The New Reality: The Report of the President's Commission on Industrial Competitiveness*, Volume I (Washington, D. C.: Superintendent of Documents, U. S. Government Printing Office, 1985) 21

14. Grace, 10.

15. "USA Snapshots," *USA Today*, 16 March 1988.

16. Dr. Ravi Batra, *The Great Depression of 1990* (New York: Simon & Schuster, 1987) 140.

17. Grace, 10.

18. Batra, 78.

19. Yoshi Tsurumi, "The Myth and Reality of Japanese Productivity," *Productivity—A National Priority* (Malibu: Pepperdine University Press, 1982) 19.

20. Daniel Yankelovich, *New Rules—Searching for Self-Fulfillment in a World Turned Upside Down* (New York: Random House, 1981) 202.

21. "USA Faces New Trade Challenge," *USA Today*, 19 April 1988.

22. "A Yen for Lending," *Inc.* (April 1988).

23. Yankelovich, 205.

24. "Productivity: A New Scenario," *Kepner-Tregoe Journal* (1981).

25. Tom Peters, *The Excellence Challenge* (Chicago: Nightingale-Conant Corporation, 1984) Audiocassette Tape 11.

26. Jan Carlzon, *Moments of Truth* (Cambridge: Ballinger Publishing Company, 1987)

27. Daniel Nelson, *Frederick W. Taylor and the Rise of Scientific Management* (Madison: The University of Wisconsin Press, 1980)

28. Anthony Smith, *The Mind* (New York: The Viking Press, 1984) 2.

29. From various talks by Dr. Morris Massey.

30. *ORC Public Opinion Index—Report to Management,* December 1982 (Princeton: Opinion Research Corp).

31. *Business Week* (4 August 1986): 49.

32. "Labor Leaders Urge New Approach to Match a Changing Workforce," *Philadelphia Inquirer,* 22 February 1985.

33. *Global Competition—The New Reality: The Report of the President's Commission on Industrial Competitiveness,* Volume I (Washington, D. C.: Superintendent of Documents, U. S. Government Printing Office, 1985).

Chapter 3 The Psychology of Employee Involvement

1. Daniel Yankelovich, *New Rules—Searching for Self-Fulfillment in a World Turned Upside Down* (New York: Random House, 1981) 152.

2. "Harvesting Energy!" *EI Network,* March 1988.

3. "A Discovery of Employee Involvement," *EI Network,* November 1988.

4. Daniel Yankelovich and John Immerwahr, *Putting the Work Ethic to Work* (New York: Public Agenda Foundation, 1983)

5. Frederick Herzberg, "One More Time—How Do You Motivate Employees?" *Harvard Business Review* (1987): 109.

6. *Pygmalion: The Theory of Self-Fulfilling Prophecy* (New York: McGraw-Hill, 1986) Film.

7. *Pygmalion*

8. Zig Ziglar, *See You at the Top* (Chicago: Nightingale-Conant Corporation, 1983) Audiocassette Tape.

9. Dr. Wayne Dyer, *How to Be a No-Limit Person* (Chicago: Nightingale-Conant Corporation, 1984) Audiocassette Tape.

10. Warren Bennis and Burt Nanus, *Leaders—Strategies for Taking Charge* (New York: Harper and Row, 1985) 70.

11. Frederick Herzberg, "Management of Hostility," *The Managerial Choice* (Homewood: Dow Jones-Irwin, 1976) 15.

Chapter 4 Resistance

1. *Recommendations for Worker Participation Programs from the Economic Policy Council* (UNA-USA) (Washington: U. S. Department of Labor, Bureau of Labor-Management Relations and Cooperative Programs, 1984).

2. "Labor Leaders Urge New Approach to Match a Changing Workforce," *Philadelphia Inquirer*, February 1985.

3. Robert E. Cole and Dennis Tachiki, "Forging Institutional Links: Making Quality Circles Work in the U. S.," *National Productivity Review* (1984).

4. Jefferson Beardsley, *Beyond Quality Circles* (Cincinnati: Association for Quality and Participation, 1986) Audiocassette Tape.

5. Tom Peters, *The Excellence Challenge* (Chicago: Nightingale-Conant Corporation, 1984) Audiocassette Tape.

6. Tom Peters, *In Search of Excellence* (Palo Alto: The Tom Peters Group, 1985) Film.

7. "Rebuilding to Survive," *Time* (16 February 1987): 45.

8. Janice A. Klein, "Why Supervisors Resist Employee Involvement," *Harvard Business Review* (September 1984).

9. "These Steelworkers Forge Success," *Philadelphia Inquirer*, 19 April 1987.

10. Raymond E. Alie, "The Middle Management Factor in Quality Circle Programs," *SAM Advanced Management Journal* (1986).

11. *ORC Public Opinion Index—Report to Management*, December 1982 (Princeton: Opinion Research Corp).

12. Peters, Audiocassette.

13. John Naisbett, *Megatrends* (New York: Warner Books, 1984) 40.

14. *Recommendations for Worker Participation Programs from the Economic Policy Council.*

15. D. L. Landen, Lecture at the Symposium on Construction Productivity (unpublished), Palo Alto, October 25, 1984.

Chapter 5 Management Support

1. Dr. Wayne Dyer, *How to Be a No-Limit Person* (Chicago: Nightingale-Conant Corporation, 1984) Audiocassette Tape.

Chapter 6 Setting Up the Process

1. *Quality Circle Facilitator Survey* (Red Bluff, CA: Quality Circle Institute, 1986).

2. *Work Worth Doing* (Capitol Heights, MD: National Audiovisual Center, 1987) Film.

Teambuilding, Inc.

In 1981, after years in construction management and performance improvement monitoring, Peter B. Grazier became involved in a unique experiment to use employee involvement and motivation concepts to improve productivity at a $50 million construction project for Monsanto Company in St. Louis, Missouri. The program, called CHAMP (Craftsmen Helping America Maximize Productivity) involved 300 craftsmen from the AFL-CIO Building and Construction Trades. The unprecedented program produced significant results that received wide acclaim within the construction industry and was heralded in many publications including the *Wall Street Journal*.

Based upon the success of this effort, in 1983, Mr. Grazier was invited to the Delaware Valley to create and administer a similar program for Public Service Electric & Gas Company in New Jersey for the final two years of construction of its Hope Creek Nuclear Generation Station. This program encompassed 7000 professional and craft workers, and met with similar success. The program and its concepts again received acclaim from such agencies as the Nuclear Regulatory Commission and the Institute for Nuclear Power Operations.

During these five years, it became clear that the concepts of employee involvement and motivation provided an answer to America's serious productivity issue. Involving all of the organization's people in improving the work seemed to produce more meaningful and dramatic results than previous management techniques. Therefore, to continue work in this field, Mr. Grazier formed Teambuilding, Inc., in June 1985.

Since that time, the company's work has involved professional and non-professional workers of electric utility, heavy manufacturing, and state government.

Corporate Philosophy and Mission

We believe that American workers have the ability and desire to create high performance organizations, and that the only way to achieve this is through their involvement. To that end, our mission is to spread this message as far as possible.

Services

Teambuilding, Inc., provides consulting and support services in management development pertaining to performance improvement through employee involvement. To receive information about the company's consulting services, training programs, resource data base, bi-monthly newsletter, or additional copies of this book, contact:

Teambuilding, Inc. • 12 Pine Lane • Chadds Ford, PA 19317
(215) 358-1961